Heirlooms

By Tina Houser

Warner Press, Inc.
Warner Press and "Warner Press" logo are trademarks of Warner Press, Inc.

Heirlooms
Passing Faith Stories to Your Grandchildren

Written by Tina Houser
Copyright ©2019 Warner Press, Inc.
All rights reserved.

Requests for information should be sent to:

Warner Press Inc
2902 Enterprise Dr
P.O. Box 2499
Anderson, IN 46013

www.warnerpress.org

Editor: Karen Rhodes
Cover Designer: Curtis Corzine
Layout: Katie Miller

ISBN: 9781684341184
Printed in the USA

Table of Contents

Introduction

Hi,

I'm Silly Grandma, and in some adult circles I'm also known as Tina Houser. Silly Grandma is an endearing, cherished title I carry because it was chosen for me by my grand-twins, Bowen and Kendall. You'll hear about them throughout this book, and also about Lucy who came along seven years after the twins. To be called "Silly" is by no means an insult. To a child, the word "silly" always means fun, and I hope that my grandkids always find me to be a fun part of their lives.

I really had no idea what grandparents were supposed to do when the twins entered the world. As I grew into the role, I watched what other grandparents were doing. One thing I noticed was that they didn't realize the spiritual impact they could have on their grandchildren. This book is my attempt at helping you, as a grandparent, acknowledge the potential that lies in your relationship with your grandchildren, and give ideas on how you can make that happen. Your faith story is the best heirloom you could leave them!

Psalm 71:18 (ESV)
So even to old age and gray hairs, O God, do not forsake me, until I proclaim your might to another generation, your power to all those to come.

In His Incredible Joy,

Silly Grandma

A Word from Two Friends

Upon hearing that I was writing this book, many friends encouraged me to move forward.

"I'm really excited that you're writing a book on grandparenting and spiritual conversations. The most influential persons in my faith life were my "Gram" and later my other grandma. They asked the right questions and encouraged me to keep a perspective that allowed me to see God at work in my life and in the world around me. My grandma was the one who threw the party for me when I asked Jesus into my heart at the age of nine. I didn't know— really know—it was a big deal. She made sure I knew it was something to celebrate!

Here's an idea: Throw a party for your grandchildren when they make a decision for Christ or are baptized. I think more grandparents need to know what an important investment they can make in their grandchildren's lives!
—Lindsey Eklund

I always emphasize my grandmother's impact on my spiritual life. My first memory of God and the Bible was when I sat with her on her porch. She told me that God had seen me in my mother's womb. Even before I started a relationship with Jesus, that thought became a foundational part of my life. When I learned that my mom and dad had me young, that people suggested she abort me, I did not doubt that even though I wasn't part of my parents' plan, I was part of God's plan. My grandmother is so special to me. To this day I go to her when I need wisdom, encouragement, and a good spiritual talk. —Gabriela Martinez

Passing on Heirlooms

Before our grandkids came along, hearing grandparents go on…and on…and on…about their grandkids was a total bore and, truthfully, it seemed like unnecessary conversation to me, torture I didn't deserve. Although I don't think I ever physically did it, inwardly I was doing a major eye-roll. Everything changes, though, when you actually get to don the title of grandparent. It's an unexpected and quite rewarding change of perspective. Now, I can proudly say that I qualify to be the president of the Obnoxious Grandparents Club, if there is such a thing.

Very close to our home, when we lived in Woodstock, Georgia, was a large Baptist church with an amazing playground facility that was open to the public. It was such an incredible playground that when I did my initial online search for "best free things to do with kids in Woodstock," the first thing listed was Kidzstock at First Baptist Church. Consequently, we frequented this park often with our grand-twins.

Normally, Kendall was the more outgoing, but on this particular day, Bowen was feeling his four-year-old confidence. My husband and I were watching them play as a team, when we noticed Bowen make a beeline toward a man we did not know. Kendall was right on his heels. Bowen stopped in front of the man, looked straight up into his face, and said, "Hi, my name Bowen. B-O-W-E-N. I'm a twin. This my sister." Then, he took off. Kendall, who had been standing right behind her brother, listening to what he said, stepped into the vacant place in front of the man, looked up at him, and then took off after her brother. Bowen then went to a woman we did not know. He stopped in front of her and said, "Hi, my name Bowen. B-O-W-E-N. I'm a twin. This my sister." When he was finished, he took off again. Kendall stepped up to the plate, looked at the woman, and again she raced after her brother without saying a word. In the next few minutes, Bowen did this exact thing three more times with his sister quietly following him. At the fifth person, Bowen recited his spiel just as he had been doing. This time, though, Kendall mustered the courage to say something. She said, "Hi, my name Kendall." Then very, very slowly she went on, "K-E-N…" followed by a long pause. When she continued, she abruptly said, "My name is longer dan his" and took off.

We all have a name. Your name is important to God, and it's important to me. When I meet you, I have a great desire to know your name. That's also a key message you want to get across to your grandchildren. God knows your grandchild's name and that child is important to Him, no matter how young or old, no matter how intellectually accelerated or developmentally challenged they are, no matter how coordinated or downright clumsy they are.

Although the story I told you may sound a little silly, please understand that stories are important—incredibly important. Since the beginning of time, man has relied on stories to communicate history of the culture and of the family. Let's talk about stories for a few minutes.

If I had told you the story I started this segment with by saying, "There was a boy and a girl," it wouldn't have been nearly as personal as me telling you their names and the relationship they have to me. Speaking someone's name makes the conversation much more personal. So, as you tell stories, include the names of the people involved to make it much more intimate and meaningful. And, say the name of your grandchild often and with tenderness.

Through stories, you find out something about storytellers—the things that are important to them, the things that frustrate them, the hilarious things they've been involved in, the places they've been, the unique experiences they've had, the embarrassing moments they've endured, and many other interesting one-of-a-kind encounters that make up the individuals they are today.

Stories get shared over and over again—sometimes to the point of being a little obnoxious. We occasionally and jokingly say at our house that our stories should be numbered. That way, we could avoid telling the entire thing, and instead simply shout out a number: "That reminds me of #39! Hahaha!" Followed by: "Oh yeah, I remember that!" Some stories just beg to be told repeatedly. They seem to connect easily to present things that are happening and may even serve as a reminder or caution when making decisions.

Good stories get shared time after time. If you're not sure about that, think about your favorite movie. How many times have you watched it? Three? Twenty-one? Sixty plus (as one of my friends admitted)? And why is that? It's because it has a great storyline. Or maybe because you can connect with what's going on. Or because it prompts you to take action. The story beckons you to watch again.

Stories are about unique things that have happened to you; they're not usually about your day-to-day routine and chores. Just think about a story you would be eager to share with someone else. It wouldn't be about your outing to the grocery store and what you found on each aisle that was on your list. That's too ordinary to bother sharing the details.

> Through stories, you find out something about storytellers...

Some stories are told just one more time for a good laugh. Others are told when you're remembering a certain person and how she or he influenced your life. Some are told as a matter of cementing the history and facts into the next generation. And, some are told to make a point—as an object lesson or illustration.

Every time there was a question about our honesty or integrity, my dad would somehow add in his personal experience of working at the corner store. When he was a young teenager, small stores were dotted throughout the neighborhoods. Many of the items you could purchase were "by the pound" and could be scooped out of large barrels—things like candy, sugar, flour, and nuts. On a regular basis, the contents of each barrel needed to be rotated and restocked. That was my dad's job—to keep the barrels full and fresh. His boss had a rule about working with the barrels. You had to whistle while you worked. As my dad poured more nuts into the barrel and shoveled them around, he'd hear his boss shout out, "Jim, I don't hear you whistling!" Immediately, my father would pucker his lips and blow out a tune. We always asked Dad why he had to whistle, to which he'd respond and finish the pointed story, "If I was whistling, then my boss knew I wasn't eating any of the candy or nuts!" The boss used this simple rule to keep my dad's integrity and honesty intact. The telling was not lost on us as we got the point of the story.

In my family there are stories of burning down bushes, falling into sinkholes, karate chopping warm butter, and roller skating up concrete steps. Your family has stories also, ones that you listen to, smile about, and pass on to the next generation.

People are constantly searching for their stories—their history. That's why sites like 23andme.com and ancestrydna.com are so popular and the show *Who Do You Think You Are?* draws so much interest. We have a great curiosity about where we came from and what our family story consists of. Yes, stories are important.

In Malachi, the last book of the Old Testament, the writer says that we look back at the stories of Moses to "remember" (Malachi 4:4). Why do we tell stories? We tell them to remember. The New Testament refers to stories in the Old Testament to remind people to remember God's faithfulness. I've been involved in children's ministry for four decades, because I want kids to remember how the people of the Bible served the One True God, and despite their human failings, God was always faithful. We learn about people of faith so we can remember how God worked. Kids need to hear about God's faithfulness in the lives of their grandparents, so they can remember in their own perplexing and decision-making times. The challenge for you is to learn lots of ways to start faith conversations with your grandchildren and take advantage of those moments when you can pass on your stories of faith. It's a huge opportunity and responsibility to pass on your faith story. Grandparents, your stories are important!

You're reading this book today because you want your grandchildren, when they are contemplating a decision, to remember YOUR story of how God was faithful in your life. You want them to remember the gospel—how God, through His Son Jesus, rescued you from being separated forever from Him, and now walks with you intimately every day. God's story is NOT finished. Each of us continues to write it each day, even when we are old and grey.

Isaiah 46:4 (NLT)
I will be your God throughout your lifetime—
until your hair is white with age.
I made you, and I will care for you.
I will carry you along and save you.

Why do stories matter so much?

You can't pinpoint why stories matter so much, because it's for an array of reasons. Let me present you with some that really hit home to me. Absorb these few suggestions and add your own. But, let each story leave its mark on you so you will grow in your desire to leave your faith story as a precious heirloom for those who come after you, especially your grandchildren.

Stories matter because they **draw out emotions**. Our hearts break for what someone went through. We laugh at an absurd decision and the consequences. We shake our heads in disgust. We feel a surge of envy or jealousy. We wish we could have been an eyewitness. Stories break through our outer crust and touch our emotions.

When you share a story and notice tears in the eyes of the hearers, you know you have reached their emotions. But it doesn't have to go that far. The raised or furled eyebrow, the hint of a smile, or an all-out belly laugh are evidence that emotions are being drawn out.

When the hearer of your story relates on an emotional level, he has made a deeper connection with what you are saying. You want your grand-children to reach this emotional point. Your story will never be boring if they do. Emotions are one of the great creations of God that fill each of us with evidence of life—love, laughter, grief—that whole fabulous roller coaster.

Stories matter because **we relate to stories.** They provide us with com-mon ground. Personal stories are full of, "Oh, I've been there" moments, "I've done that" reactions, and "I'm not the only one who ever thought about that" realizations. They connect us. Stories take people from think-ing they have nothing in common to realizing they have plenty to share. Oh my! That's what you want to achieve with your grandchildren. You yearn for common ground that will connect you to this person two gen-erations removed, who lives in a culture that you struggle to understand. Common ground seems so distant sometimes, but your stories can bridge the gap that feels extremely wide.

When you feel at a loss to understand the things your grandchildren are talking about, especially as their culture relates to technology, inten-tionally spend time learning (video games, texting, video chat, emojis, shows they watch, etc.). Challenge yourself, and then commit to follow-ing through on learning something new that will help you communicate with your grandchildren. Enjoy letting them introduce those things to you, praise them for their incredible knowledge and flexibility, and then do your best to integrate what you have learned into your daily living.

Your stories of the past are invaluable, but your ability to be up-to-date (at least somewhat) and engaged in the present world carries a clear message also. You don't have to be the "hip" grandparent, but just move into the present century. Enter their world without being obnoxious about it.

> Stories take people from thinking they have nothing in common to realizing they have plenty to share.

Stories matter because they **help answer questions**. When did that happen? Why did they move? Where were you when that took place? How old were they? Is that why…? How did you react? How did you get through that? What happened next?

Just last night we gathered around the dinner table with our son and his family (three grandchildren). The conversation somehow led to a string of stories that had to do with the experimental radiation treatment I went through 35 years ago at Stanford University. After I explained the most basic details of the main story, both Bowen and Kendall burst forth with questions.

"How old was Daddy when that happened?" (2½ years old) "Why did they put tattoos on you?" (My mother used a ruler and marker to connect the tattoo dots each morning. That told the doctors where to place the blocks so they knew where to put the radiation.) "How long did it take?" (I went every day, Monday through Friday, for six weeks. It was a couple of hours each day.)

I had told them that I'd lost 27 pounds in that six weeks, so one of the questions they asked was, "Did you throw up all the time?" Yes, I did. In fact, one morning I was so sick I didn't think I could make it the half-mile from our apartment to the hospital without throwing up. So, I gave your daddy a big pot out of the kitchen cabinet to carry with him. We got on the elevator, along with a very well-dressed woman. She looked down at your daddy with a smile and said, "Are you playing with the kettle?"

Your daddy very matter-of-factly answered, "No. This is in case my mommy barfs." Taken aback by his answer, the lady immediately started staring at the elevator number panel. The grandkids loved that part of the story, and it answered their question. The entire experience of having total lymphoid irradiation was filled with God's intervention to provide for us. Through the stories, many of their questions got answered.

Stories matter because they **explain why a person is who he is**. Stories of what it was like growing up, or stories that describe a terrifying experience often help you understand "why" a person acts the way she does or "why" he has a unique perspective on one particular thing. *When our son was about eight, we regularly attended a home life group. The people who hosted the group had rescued a Doberman pincher from an abusive situation. The children of all the adults in the group played while we talked, and Roxie (the dog) would usually play along with them. For some reason, one night, Roxie sprang up and chomped her teeth around our son's mouth and chin, ripping a long slash in his face.* When we told that story to the grandkids, they put two and two together and understood why, even though their daddy loves big dogs, he absolutely detests Dobermans. The story explained why he is who he is.

Another story that helps explain why someone is who he is involves my father-in-law. *He was an unexpected addition to his family, which already consisted of seven children. Apparently, it was too much for his father, so he walked out on the family, leaving a single mom to raise eight kids. My father-in-law never knew his father, and it affected his self-image greatly. It was obvious that he carried the blame for their family falling apart, even though he had nothing to do with being born.* Knowing that part of his story helps explain some of Great-Grandpa's actions and attitudes.

Stories matter because **children LOVE stories**! We all love stories! When you have dinner with someone, sharing amazing stories makes for a wonderful evening. So, play into the natural love of stories and tell your grandkids the true story of how God took your old sinful self and made you a new creation. Wow them with stories of God's faithfulness in your life.

Your grandchildren want to hear your story. They are fascinated to hear how God has worked or is working in the life of someone they know and love. It's not always the grandparents who do the initiating, though, in order to share their story. My grandkids are constantly asking my husband and me to tell them a story. We don't usually have to talk them into it. When they were little, we used the time in the car to tell stories. That has now become the natural time to request a story. We share stories of how times were different, and we share stories of how God has made us different because of His grace shown through His Son, Jesus.

The Bible points out examples of the "old people"—the grandparents. Even if they weren't blood relation, they interacted as grandparents and grandchildren: Barnabas took Mark under his wing, Moses taught Joshua, Elizabeth helped Mary. In these three examples, the person in the grandparent role took the initiative to pour into these younger people. But, it's not just the desire of the grandparents that provides the opportunity to share a story. There are also biblical examples where the grandchildren asked for the stories to be passed on. They wanted to be recipients of this faith…of this blessing…of this life in Christ. Elisha (the one in the grandchild role) asked for a double portion from Elijah. Ruth (the one in the grandchild role) said to Naomi, "Where you go I will go, and where you stay, I will stay. Your people will be my people and your God my God" (Ruth 1:16, NIV). Recognize that your grandchildren really do want to know your story. We all have the desire to be part of a good story, and that includes your grandchildren.

Faith stories matter because **they indicate that God did not stop moving** in the lives of His people after the "Amen" of Revelation 22:21. You don't want to only recall from decades past, but you want to share faith stories from this past week. Be excited about what God is doing today. Understanding this will help kids grasp that we serve a real God.

> Faith stories matter because they indicate that God did not stop moving in the lives of His people...

On one occasion my husband was unable to accompany me on a speaking engagement, one where I had to change planes at the Minneapolis airport. It's huge! That meant I would have to carry my computer bag and banner, along with my travel purse, through the airport. At this point in my life, walking any distance was difficult, but carrying things was super painful. Before I left home, I asked my grandkids to pray with me about this potentially difficult situation, which they gladly did.

The plane landed in Minneapolis and I felt all my muscles tense as I prepared to leave the plane and make the trek to the other end of the airport for my connecting flight. As I walked through the waiting area, I looked up to see a pink transport cart. A little woman with white hair was the driver. She motioned to me and sweetly said, "Would you like a ride?" I hadn't reserved a ride. She didn't know who I was. But, out of this crowd of people, she made eye contact with me, like I was the only person de-boarding. I recognized that God was providing my help, and I whispered as I took steps toward the pink cart, "Thank You, Jesus." This wasn't just a regular black, seats-torn, transport cart. This one was pink, bedazzled with sparkles, and driven by a little lady who looked like the fairy godmother from Cinderella. As the cart moved its way down the corridors, I looked from side to side and people were smiling at the cart. I overheard one little girl say, "Oh Daddy, look. It's a princess." (I was real tempted to do a parade wave.) Several more times, I heard gasps from little girls and similar exclamations. Not only had God provided me a way to get through the airport without the pain of lugging all my stuff, but He created a special memory by making me feel like a princess.

I couldn't wait to get home to share with my grandchildren, especially Kendall who was really into the Disney princesses at the time, the way God answered our prayer. I got to share how God intersected my life that very week. It wasn't something I remembered from long ago, but it was God walking with me right now. These may be the most important stories to share with your grandchildren, so they know the God you speak of is the God of NOW.

Your Spiritual Story

In order for you to be able to tell your spiritual story, you have to know what it is. More than likely, you have never intentionally spent time thinking about all the different pieces that have impacted your story— how you came to invite God to lead your life and how God has worked in your life on a daily basis. Being intentional is extremely important. You have to think about it, and I mean more than a minute or two. Otherwise, the opportunities to share with your grandchildren will come and go…and it won't happen. You'll be thumping yourself in the forehead afterwards when you realize the door was open and you didn't take advantage of walking through it with your grandchildren. It wasn't because you were scared. It wasn't because you doubted that they would be interested. It was because you just hadn't thought it through. Without being intentional, the opportunities will go unnoticed.

Sharing your spiritual story is not just one sit-down-let's-talk time. The idea is not to bombard your grandchildren with your life story, from birth to present. It's about breaking it down so that each little piece packs a punch. Each little piece turns their eyes to Jesus, and they get one more glimpse of how their life could be different by totally submitting to Him. Every single day…or at least every moment you spend time with your grandchildren…is an opportunity to give them a little bit more of your story.

Your spiritual story is made up of many chapters, and each one can be told at a different time and in different ways. Don't feel rushed to cram it all in, but don't neglect it either. Work on creating a mindset that your goal for each time you spend with one grandchild, or all of them together, will be to intentionally point them to Jesus by sharing at least a tidbit of your spiritual story.

Your salvation story is a big important chapter and should be one that is thought through, so you can tell it the best way possible. How did God take you from a place of disobedience to a place where you recognized that He loved you so much He offered His Son Jesus as the way to bring you back to Him? How did that happen? What did it look like in your life? Granted, you could probably do a day-long seminar on the subject, but I'm afraid the attention span of your grandchild isn't sufficient for that (no matter how much you love each other).

Condensing it without leaving out the key components is a challenge. So, wrap your head around this idea: If you and your grandchild stepped inside an elevator and you pushed the button for the twelfth floor—you had a 12-story ride on the elevator together—would you be able to tell your grandchild about your salvation during that ride? What would you say? What would you include? This is your big opportunity. Make sure you're prepared and intentional about it! You don't want to crash and burn because you didn't feel it was important enough for some preparation.

It's critical for your grandkids to understand that admitting your sin, accepting Jesus as your Savior, and making Him the daily Lord of your life is a heart issue, a surrender, a lifestyle, a mindset, and a journey that happens 24/7/365. They need to know that you are involved in this continual journey with the Lord. It's not a one-time event. It's not something you have checked off your bucket list. It's a to-death-and-beyond relationship.

And if you have a questioning grandchild who has an argumentative nature, your faith story is a way to settle that spirit within him or her because it happened to you. It's not someone else's recollections you're imparting. They can't argue with what you experienced—the change you underwent because you accepted God's gift of salvation. Your grandchildren may want to argue with you about theology, what a denomination observes, or how a Greek word is translated, but they can't argue with you about what has happened—who you used to be and who you are now because of Christ.

If you're going to be intentional, that means you need to prepare. Here's a suggestion that's helped me lead many others through this process. You're going to list the events that were spiritual markers for you.

So, get yourself a big pad of sticky-back notes. On separate notes, write each time God obviously rocked your world. Include times when you were sure that God stepped in and maybe went so far as to change your life course. Do this randomly, and don't attempt to put the sticky notes in any order at this point. As you complete each one, stick it to a blank wall, the side of the refrigerator, a piece of poster board…you get the idea.

Doesn't it always happen that when you want to recall something, it seems to hide in your brain where you can't grab it? These prompting questions may help bring specific spiritual memories to the top and out of hiding. So, start talking to yourself and ask…

- How would my life have been different if I had not received Jesus as my Savior?

- Apart from my actual salvation experience, at what moment did I feel closest to God?

- Who is my favorite faithful person in the Bible? Why? This reveals who you connect with most easily and tells something about your own story. *I love the story of Caleb! He and Joshua were the only two who courageously spied out the Promised Land and excitedly recommended the Israelites move in to the land God wanted to give them. The other 10 spies were frightened by the huge people—giants—in the land. Consequently, the Israelites wandered around the desert for 40 more years. That entire time, Caleb prepared himself to take on the giants. Can't you just imagine this 80-year-old man doing push-ups and lifting weights to be ready for battle? With each curl, I can imagine Caleb muttering to himself, "I'm gonna get me some giants. Bring 'em on. You're going down, giants." When the Israelites finally entered the Promised Land, and Joshua was now in charge, Joshua gave Caleb first choice of what part of the land he wanted. Caleb could've chosen the lush lands by the rivers that would've made life easier, but no-o-o-o. He chose the land of the giants! I want to be like Caleb…prepared for the big challenges…not intimidated to stare down the giants and dare them to come against God Almighty who lives within me…not afraid of risks…placing my hope in God. I want my grandchildren to see very clearly that I possess qualities like Caleb.*

- When you had a crisis—something that turned your world upside down—when did your heart cry, "Help!"? When have you cried out for help? *There was a time when the doctors gave me no hope to walk again. I was confined to a wheelchair, fighting an out-of-control infection in my leg. Our son was six at the time and didn't see the wheelchair as part of our future. One day he stood in another room of my parents' farmhouse, about 20 feet from me, and put his arms straight out in front of him. With a serious and demanding look on his face, he said, "Mommy, walk to me." His extended arms beckoned me to try, and his insistence filled me with hope. My heart was screaming out to the Lord, "Help me!" Even though I saw no good outcome to it, I raised myself to a standing position in front of the chair. Cautiously, I took one small step...and...fell flat on my face. I had tried, and because of this little towhead's faith, I tried again and again. When the next appointment came up on my calendar, I walked into the examining room unassisted!* This is part of my spiritual story, and it's one I recall when I think of times I've cried out to God for help.

Oh my, what a hodge-podge of free-thinking. It's best to do this over a period of a couple of days or even a week, because now that you have informed your brain what it should be looking for, it will recall the events at strange, unconnected times.

Once you have completed your initial brainstorming and have this huge collection of sticky notes, it's time to arrange them in sequence. As you share each of these stories with your grandchildren, you more than likely won't share them in order, but it's good for you to see the journey God has led you on so far. That journey comes alive when you put the events in chronological order.

How and When Do You Tell a Piece of Your Story?

First, you need to find the right time. If your grandkids are engrossed in a movie, running through the house on a sugar high, or exhausted, it's just not the right time. If you keep these hints in mind, it will assist you in being intentional.

Some of our most special times of sharing spiritual stories have been when the grandkids spend the night. At the close of the day when we're all winding down, part of the routine is to share something about my God-journey with them. In a calm, sincere voice before reading a book they have chosen, I say, "This is one of my favorite times. Each time I'm with you, I thank God that He decided to give you to me as grandchildren. It's one of my biggest blessings. I think God said, 'Hey, I'm going to take Bowen and Kendall (say their name[s]) and make them Tina's grandkids.'" It always starts that way for us, because it invites God into our conversation.

You create a more intimate atmosphere when you sit next to them. No matter the age of your grandchild, the closer you can physically be to him or her, the better. For grandparents who have a chasm of miles that separate you from your grandchild, please don't discount the power of Skype and Facetime. The technology may intimidate you somewhat, but my words to you are, "Get over it!" It may seem a little "artificial" to you, but it's completely natural for them, and they really don't understand why you're not comfortable with talking to a screen.

Take your time. One of the unique aspects of being a grandparent is that you don't have to feel hurried. The rush that comes with a frantic schedule just isn't there. You can take a deep breath and simply enjoy each other's company. That's when those moments of telling faith stories happen. If you know your grandkids, then you know when the "rest of the story" needs to happen (depending on the age of your kids). Because you've created a more relaxed environment, there's plenty of time to ask questions!

In these conversations, be honest and authentic. Your grandkids have enough people in their lives who are putting on fronts and pretending to be someone they aren't. They've become very skilled at spotting a fake. That should be a loud warning to you to be truthful in all you say.

Even though it's tempting to go down rabbit trails, letting one story lead you to another unrelated one, commit to being concise. You're telling this particular story for a specific reason. If your grandkids are curious enough to ask questions, then by all means entertain them, but always keep the point in view. Remember, if you're being intentional, there will be time to share the rest of your story.

A big aspect of being intentional is figuring out how to go from a casual ordinary experience or conversation into telling your faith story. Decide how each part will be told. The next section of this book gives you lots of ideas on how you can do precisely that.

You have a story. Your story is important. It's important to you, it's important to the people you meet, it's important to your family, and it is incredibly important to your grandchildren. It is a cherished heirloom you are passing on to them. An heirloom is something of great value that you pass on. God created your journey to be unique so that you could share it. When you share your faith stories with your grandchildren, they see into your soul and realize the faith you have in Jesus is of great value to you. It's worth passing on.

I have lots of stories, but the most important ones have to do with my relationship with my Savior and Lord, Jesus. Envision a 1000-piece puzzle with me. This puzzle represents how God has infiltrated your life in all these different ways. When you pull out one piece, it represents just one of the stories of your faith journey. It is just one piece to the puzzle that is your life. Each time you share one of your stories with your grandchildren, they connect the pieces, and the puzzle makes a little more sense. You give them a better picture of who God is.

The desire of my heart in writing this book is that sharing your faith stories with your grandchildren will become a natural part of your relationship with them.

I'm sure God delights in being part of the time you spend with your precious grandkids.

> You have a story. Your story is important. It's important to you... and it is incredibly important to your grandchildren. It is a cherished heirloom you are passing on to them.

Wouldn't it be wonderful to hear God say to your grandchild the words that Paul penned? *I remember your genuine faith, for you share the faith that first filled your grandmother Lois (insert your name) and your mother, Eunice. And I know that same faith continues strong in you* (2 Timothy 1:5, NLT).

The Impact of Grandparents

One hundred fifty years ago, it wasn't uncommon to see multi-generations living under the same roof, with grandparents seamlessly stepping in to help raise their grandchildren. Then, our country went through a time when the nuclear family lived separate from the grandparents, as each became more independent. Now, it appears that grandparents are back in the picture with a more influential role in their grandkids' lives. In fact, the number of children being raised by their grandparents has doubled since 1970, now sitting at 2.7 million grandparents raising their grandchildren.* Three big reasons for the shift are:

- Financial. Older people find it difficult to meet the financial obligations of living on their own, and it's extremely expensive for parents to afford childcare for each of their kids. Grandparents step in to provide childcare for 30% of children under the age of five whose mothers work.

- Addictions, especially opioid addiction, have skyrocketed. Along with addiction comes incarceration and neglect...and many times the children are taken away from the parent(s) and put into foster care.

- The foster care system is overloaded. For whatever reason a child is in foster care, the statistics show that 25 kids are being raised by a grandparent (or relative) for each child who is in foster care. That's staggering! It points out how important grandparents are in our society today.

> ...Statistics show that 25 kids are being raised by a grandparent (or relative) for each child who is in foster care.

*Information according to the article, "23 Statistics on Grandparents Raising Grandchildren" (May 22, 2017). For the article, the writer, Brandon Gaille, gathered information from AARP.org, MetLife.com, Pew-Internet.org, and the U.S. Census 2010.

What happens when a grandparent is the sole provider?

We have this stereotypical idea of what a grandparent looks like. If you were to draw a caricature of a grandma, she would probably have white hair up in a bun, an apron on, little wire-rimmed glasses, and either be stirring something at the stove or lounging in her rocking chair. Grandparents don't come close to that today! Now, ask an elementary-age-child to draw a picture or describe in words what a grandmother looks like. This depiction will be quite different. Grandma may be meeting with clients at her law firm, working out at the gym, raising chickens as a hobby, volunteering at a food bank, on a medical education tour in Kenya, or just about anything. There's no longer one mental picture that depicts a grandma. This older generation is still healthy, vibrant, and involved. Legacyproject.org reports that the average age for a woman to become a grandma is 50 years old.

Most people have an idea, or maybe even a dream, about what their life will look like when they're 50 or 60. The kids will be raised and on their own. They can sleep in, go to bed early, go to bed late...whatever they please. They'll finally get to travel and see parts of the world they've always been fascinated with. Income from retirement benefits, Social Security, and bank accounts give them comfort that all the bills will be paid.

For many grandparents, life changes in a moment. When a grandparent takes on the responsibility of being the main or sole caretaker for a grandchild (or grandchildren, in many cases), pretty much all the plans they made for their last 40 years come to a halt. The mental picture they had of how they would live the last season of their life is almost unrecognizable.

Grandparents take on the role of the parent, but they're not prepared physically, emotionally, socially, or financially. God created man and woman to have children young in life for a reason. Parenting takes a lot of energy. You can't assume that a grandparent has that same amount of energy. Let's be truthful here. Your body can't do what it used to do; you just don't have the oomph or strength you once had. Things change drastically when you become a custodial grandparent. You're now keeping little ones on a napping schedule and getting older ones up early to prepare for school. What happened to sleeping in? Kids need to be taken to and picked up from practices, school events, and church programs. There's running, loud noises, video game sound effects, craziness, and all-out fights between siblings throughout your home, and it's not just now and then (so you have time to recover). No, it's all the time! What happened to quietly reading a book? The money that was going to take you to exotic places of your dreams now goes to pay for clothing, food, birthday party gifts, team fees, and special activities. There's a group at church composed of common-age friends you have been part of for years. Now, when they meet, you have to consider whether or not you can attend, depending on finding a babysitter. Providing childcare isn't the norm for most churches when it comes to senior activities. With so many custodial grandparents, it may be time for the church to re-evaluate.

Yes, it's hard, and the timing doesn't seem right, but the role you play in raising your grandchildren will impact their entire lives. If you're a custodial grandparent, I'm praying for you to find the positive in each day and to rely on God to take care of your needs in creative ways. If you're reading this and totally do not relate, then join me in praying for your fellow grandparents in this position. Look around and identify any custodial grandparents among your acquaintances. Take notice of how you might be able to assist them in the daily tasks of this new role.

Grandparent, You Are Important!

No matter what the particular situation is with your grandchildren, I want to assure you that you are extraordinarily important to them. You may be miles apart and only give one another physical hugs every other year. Family tensions may make you question what you're able to do with your grandkids. Divorce brings a different dynamic to grandparenting, where you find yourself vying for any opportunity to be part of your grandchild's life. Let me encourage you in this: Don't doubt for a moment that God wants you to be a valuable part of your grandchild's life.

The relationship between you and your grandchildren is the second most important relationship in that child's emotional development. The only impact more powerful comes from the relationship the child has with the parents. Grandparenting may be the only thing I love being number two at. But, if you're in the position of being the main caretaker, you just moved into first place. So, grandparents, you have a big, important stake in your grandchild's life. It's of life and death importance. Stop for a moment and say this OUT LOUD, inserting the name of each one of your grandchildren. "God made me important to _____." Pretty simple. I hope you really heard yourself.

There is a common story I hear among grandparents. They've been left brokenhearted when their adult children have walked away from their faith and the church. These troubled grandparents feel like they somehow messed up with their own children, and now it's out of their hands—there's nothing they can do to claim their grandchildren for Jesus. How far from the truth! This is your second chance. This is a do-over for you. God is giving you another chance to do as Psalm 71:18 (ESV) says: *So even to old age and gray hairs, O God, do not forsake me, until I proclaim your might to another generation, your power to all those to come.*

If your grandchildren are not being raised by Christian parents, you have the opportunity of your lifetime, because your field is ripe for the harvest (John 4:35). One of your biggest steps will be realizing that you, and sometimes you alone, can take your grandchildren's hands and lead them into eternity with Jesus. That's worth taking a risk. That's worth spending some time in thought as to how you can be intentional. The psalmist reminds us in Psalm 78:4 (ESV), *We will not hide them from their children but tell to the coming generation the glorious deeds of the LORD, and his might, and the wonders that he has done.*

If your grandkids are not being exposed to a healthy church family, then take the initiative and host a sleepover on a Saturday night. Taking them to church with you on Sunday morning seems a natural part of that sleepover. Think of the times when you get a call asking, "Can you watch the kids?" as an invitation to introduce your grandkids to Jesus and help them fall in love with God's Word. If you do this on a regular basis, living out your faith in front of them, praying that God will honor and bless your efforts, I have to believe that on the day you stand at heaven's door, God will say, "Well done, My good and faithful grandparent."

You are important as the chain breaker. Behaviors get passed down from parents to children, whether they realize it or not. Those behaviors can be positive or negative. Children growing up in a home where husband and wife disrespect one another with harsh words will naturally think that using harsh words is the way to express themselves when their opinion differs. In the same light as with parents, be careful as a grandparent not to make the negative things that have been said to you or done to you part of the heirlooms you leave your grandkids. *My father-in-law, Veryle, had five older brothers. They physically fought for their single mom's attention. They also expressed their love for one another through extreme rough-housing. I got a taste of that on my very first encounter with Veryle. I was at my fiancé's apartment awaiting the arrival of his parents. When the doorbell rang, Ray was busy, so I excitedly went to answer it. As I swung the door open, I faced a tall man with his fist raised high in the air, ready to clobber me. You could tell he was ready to let someone have it. When he saw it was me, his fist slowly dropped to his side and he didn't seem to know what to do. During that same visit, Veryle repeatedly grabbed my head and pulled it down, so he could clutch me in his armpit. Then, he proceeded to take his knuckles and grind them into my scalp. It hurt…really hurt…to the point of tears. When I asked Ray why his dad kept doing that to me, Ray informed me that it was his dad's way of saying that he liked me. I quickly responded, "Then tell him not to like me anymore!"* That was inappropriate behavior, but that's all Veryle knew growing up. Yes, Ray talked with his dad and I never got another "Dutch-rub," in spite of the fact that Veryle was very fond of his new daughter-in-law.

> ...Be careful as a grandparent not to make the negative things that have been said to you or done to you part of the heirlooms you leave your grandkids.

Be aware of what's being passed on to your grandchildren and what you want your heirlooms to be. I'm beyond the flighty time in my life. As I think about eternity for Bowen, Kendall, and Lucy, I want to be very intentional about where I put my time and energy at this point.

Special Grandparent Words

While you contemplate your role as a grandparent, some words may take on a new, or more complete, meaning. Exploring these words can help you be a better grandparent. More than anything else, absorbing these words as your "grandparent banner" points out how the relationship with your grandchild is different from the parent-child relationship or a relative-child relationship.

"Because"

"Experiences"

"Together"

"Watch"

"With"

Five special grandparent words!

"Because"
At Christmastime, grandparents tend to stuff the underside of the tree with gift upon gift for grandchildren. I don't know about you, but it gets a little ridiculous (and somewhat embarrassing) at our house. On birthdays, grandparents gather around to watch the flames on the candles be blown out. It may be tradition to spend the Fourth of July at the lake, chowing down on picnic foods and twirling sparklers in the air. An intentional stop at Grandma's house on Halloween to display the creative costume and get a "special" treat is a must. If your grandchildren live close to you, or even if they don't, I'm sure you have expected things you do throughout the year.

But what if you did the unexpected? What if you did something just "because?" What if you interrupted their lives for a moment in order to show your grandchildren they truly have a special place in your life, that they are more than part of the tradition of holidays?

"Because" is an interesting word that grandparents can take advantage of. Who else could show up and "kidnap" the kids to drive around and look at Christmas lights? Or take them to the grocery store to choose their favorite frozen ice cream candy bar? Or go to a movie? You can do those **because** you're a grandparent. Parents aren't afraid of their children being whisked away **because** they're in your care. These unexpected events provide a conversation starter if you take a moment to be intentional about what you're doing.

Your conversation starter might sound something like this: "I didn't tell you what was going on, and that certainly reminds me of how God doesn't always tell us what life is going to be like. I think God enjoys doing the unexpected, and I know that it makes Him happy when I rely on Him no matter what circumstance I'm in the middle of."

Don't abuse the status, though. You don't want to get away with breaking rules that Mom and Dad have set, just **because** "Oh, it's Grandpa." That's not teaching grandkids respect. I try...and I've got to admit it's difficult sometimes...to stick with Mom and Dad's expectations. The cookie jar has always been open territory at our house as long as I can remember. You were on your own to decide how much you would gorge yourself. But, the grand-twins have other rules at home—one treat a day. I do my best to honor that rule when they are in my care. And I've got to admit, the kids have been extremely honest about whether or not they have already had their treat for the day. I was astonished when Kendall once said, "I've had a treat today, but Bowen hasn't, so he can have one." I knew that at special times of the year, though—like at Christmas, Halloween, and Valentine's Day—those rules got stretched a bit at home. So, I felt comfortable indulging them just a bit more, seasonally. I don't want them to think that there's one set of rules for home and another set at their grandparents' house. That would be abusing **because.**

In many ways, I think **because** gifts and side-trips are more meaningful than the ones that are pretty much expected. **Because** gifts happen when you're out and you see something that reminds you of one grandchild. It could be something as simple as a purple Sharpie marker, because your grandchild loves the color purple. When you present this **because** gift, you say, "I saw this, and it made me think of you."

Bowen had his hair cut in a mohawk, just like a friend, but his mohawk just didn't turn out right when he did it himself. So, when the boys appeared together in a play, the friend's mother helped the boys quickly get out of their costumes and made their hair presentable again. She brought Gorilla Snot. (Yes, you read that correctly…snot!) Bowen was quite happy with the results and had everyone he came in contact with stroke through the soft spikes. I browsed through the hair products at the discount store, and there it was— Gorilla Snot. For $3 I made my grandson feel special. I'm not sure I actually said, "I saw this snot and thought of you," though.

You don't have to get every grandchild something. Get past trying to make things even. In fact, I don't think that's healthy. Make sure you do similar little **because** gifts for the others at other times, which will make them feel extra special to you at their particular time.

Because gifts and experiences help build a bond of trust with your grandchildren. They serve as a little reminder that you love them all the time and you think about them all the time. I have to believe that it makes a difference when the time comes that they need a trusted person to talk to, who loves them unconditionally. Do something for your grandchild today…just **because.**

Some **because** gifts or experiences I could provide for my grandkids are:

1. _____

2. _____

3. _____

"Experiences"
Think back on all the Christmases and birthdays. One or two gifts over those years will stand out as something special. What you most likely remember is the experience of being together, the people who were there, and the sense of belonging because someone made you feel special.

My grandkids, probably just like yours, spend a day around Thanksgiving time cleaning out their closets and the basement of toys they've outgrown or just no longer want. Many of them have hardly been played with. Gladly, I can say that they donate them, so they'll become a gift for another child whose family can't afford the brand new one. Why are they going through their toys? To make room for the new ones that will find their home there on Christmas morning.

Extravagant hardly describes the pile of wrapped gifts under the tree. In the midst of paper flying in all directions, one more gift from me seems to get lost in the wrappings. Later in the day, the grandkids may take some time to see how it works or cuddle up with it for a few minutes, but mostly it gets lost in the craziness.

I've started giving gifts that concentrate more on memories instead of opening a package. I've started giving experiences. There's still the excitement of wrapping the unknown, and part of the fun is in the creative way I unveil the experience. When you give experiences, many times that means getting to try something for the very first time, which leads to lots of interesting conversations. Think about giving something that you can do together, rather than something that separates them into their own little world.

A couple of years ago, I gave the twins and Big Pa a gift for the three of them together. It was tickets for a one-hour plane ride over our area in a single-engine, 4-seater, private plane. Surprisingly, the cost was no more than buying them three individual gifts. Every time I have the twins in the car and we drive past the airport, it never fails that one of them will say, "That's where we went up in the airplane with Big Pa." But, that's never the end of the conversation. They go on to describe what they saw and how they felt. (Kendall was not as at ease with the flight as Bowen was.) Bowen always wraps it up with, "I'd like to do that again." Never would they talk that long about a toy they had received. And, the experience will be a memory of their grandpa they will cherish the rest of their lives...long after he has run on ahead to wait for them in heaven.

Experiences draw us closer, so that when grandkids have decisions to make or are going through a challenging time, they will comfortably approach grandparents for advice and a listening ear.

Another experience we've given is a 90-minute pass to the trampoline park. We've done this twice, with about two years in between. The time lapse made for some extremely positive ways to articulate observations of how they had grown and developed. Kids love to hear how much they've changed and im-

proved. These times when you can point out how they've grown, don't forget to verbally acknowledge your thanksgiving to God that your grandchildren are healthy enough to enjoy such an activity.

Experiences draw us closer...

The other special thing about giving experiences for Christmas* or birthdays is that it moves the gift away from the day. You're not going to use the tickets on Christmas Day or during a birthday party. It's an excuse to extend the celebration and make one more day of it. Instead of it getting lost in the chaos of all the other gifts and things that are going on that day, the gift gets extra special attention when the day for the experience actually arrives. It's a double anticipation. There's the anticipation and countdown until Christmas or a birthday, and then you have another countdown until you get to go do what you have planned together.

When you give experiences as gifts, you set yourself up for an opportunity to provide encouragement to your grandchild.

Another experience gift was an archery pass. We have an archery facility in our town where kids and adults can receive instruction in this unique sport. But they also have "free time" when anyone can come in to shoot arrows at the bullseye. There are instructors available to give tips to anyone wishing to get that kind of assistance. Archery is a sport that very few kids are involved in, but it is really a fun experience for those who are naturally coordinated and love anything that has to do with sports. Be ready to use this experience to step into a conversation about how you have hit God's bullseye sometimes and done exactly what He wanted you to do. And, then again, there are times when you have not hit the mark and failed to live the way God would want you to.

It's going to take some research on your part to discover unique experiences in your area. The gift experiences I share with you are not necessarily available in your area, so take these ideas and see what similar type experiences are within your reach. Surf the net to see about indoor rock-climbing parks, plays, ballets, animal exhibits, or night walks at the zoo. Now, you have the creative juices flowing!

*Check out the "12 Socks of Christmas" on page 106 for experience ideas specifically for Christmas time.

Some experiences I could plan with my grandchildren:

1. _____

2. _____

3. _____

"Together"

Although it feels like a challenge sometimes to enter the world of your grandchildren, you must be diligent about understanding their language and building a relationship. That can't happen unless you're together in one form or another. To find that common ground, endeavor to find things you can do together. You don't want it to be so complicated that you can't have a conversation in the midst of the activity. The complexity also depends on the skills and age of your grandchild.

It's so easy to let your grandchildren retreat into the video world and disengage from the people around them. One day an incident occurred that made me think a little deeper about how people perceive video games. *I enthusiastically said, "Let's do something together, Bowen." He contemplated for just a second and then suggested video games. I responded that I don't play them, and I really wanted to do something together. He didn't pause a moment in the conversation when he said, "But you always say you love to watch me play." He really thought that was a way to be together. I found it especially odd, because Bowen is one of those kids who gets so focused that he doesn't hear anything going on around him.* How could he seriously think we were doing something **together** when we were playing video games?

From that encounter I became aware that I needed to be more intentional and have something in mind. Rather than opening it up to any ideas, I needed to have two or three options for him to pick from (none of which would be video games) that would accomplish **togetherness.**

I love **together** activities! Memories are made when we're **together.**

Build something together.

Building doesn't have to be with hammer, nails, and wood. If that is not your cup of tea, then think about building with PVC. My husband and I are not at all handy with building anything, but a nifty little gadget that's made us both feel successful is a PVC cutter. It ratchets around the pipe—1 pump…2 pumps…3 pumps…and you have a clean cut. *Big Pa and Bowen put together a stand-up sandbox for 20-month-old Lucy. The structure is made out of PVC, and a plastic storage tub fits into it to hold the sand (or water or anything you want it to hold). And, there's a lid! I peeked into the garage to see one of them measuring the PVC while the other used the tool. I can't tell you the pride the two of them felt when my daughter-in-law requested that they make her one for her classroom.*

You don't have to take on a big project (although the PVC project only took a little more than an hour). You can build something out of Legos. The important thing is that you do it **together.** On a cautionary note, be careful not to separate the pieces of the activity so that each person is doing their own thing. Keep it **together.**

> # Memories are made when we're together.

Make dinner together.
Depending on the age and skill, you can prepare a dinner that is as complicated as you'd like. This is the perfect time to tell stories about when you ate this meal, who originally prepared it, and what significance it has to you.

I invited Kendall to help me prepare a dinner of lasagna for our families. I pulled the Betty Crocker Cookbook *that had been a wedding present off the shelf and lovingly opened it. The red cookbook now has worn edges, and the binding is struggling to stay together. Page 292, the lasagna recipe, is splotched with tomato sauce and unidentified drippings. I laughed as I shared with my granddaughter how this was pretty much the only recipe I used out of this cookbook, but I used it a lot when we were first married. When there's just two of you eating from a big pan of lasagna, it takes a week to get through it. As soon as the pan was empty, I'd make more…because that's the only recipe I had mastered. Then, I told her that her grandpa really loved me, because he kept eating it night after night. One day, he very gingerly expressed that he was growing tired of the lasagna, but he was so careful not to hurt my feelings.*

The lasagna recipe was a perfect one for making **together**, because it's a matter of layering. From 2-year-olds to grown grandchildren, it's a great recipe to do **together**.

If you're going to cook **together**, my advice is to make a recipe that consists of layering. That keeps everything simple enough that you can be **together**. Let me just throw out two other recipes that are homeruns for being **together** with your grandkids.

7-Layer Cookies

- 1 stick margarine, melted
- 1½ c. graham crackers, fine crumbs
- 1 small can coconut
- 1 6-oz. package semi-sweet chocolate chips
- 1 6-oz. package butterscotch chips
- 1 c. pecans, chopped fine
- 1 can sweetened condensed milk

Melt the margarine in a 9" x 13" glass pan. Rub the sides of the pan with the margarine to keep the cookies from sticking. Then add your layers. Sprinkle in: graham cracker crumbs, chocolate chips, butterscotch chips, coconut, and pecans. Drizzle the sweetened condensed milk over the entire pan. Bake at 350° for 25-30 minutes. After 2 minutes, take a spatula around the edges to loosen the cookie from the pan. (Don't wait any longer than that.) Let them completely cool and then cut.

Okay, that was the goodies. Now for a good hearty recipe.

Ham and Cheese Wreath

- 2 cans crescent rolls
- 1 c. mozzarella cheese
- ½ c. pepperoncinis
- ¼ t. dried basil
- 1/3 lb. salami
- 1/3 lb. ham
- ¼ lb. prosciutto
- 6 slices provolone cheese cut in halves

Preheat the oven to 375°. Cover a large cookie sheet with parchment paper. Place a 5"-6" bowl in the center. Unroll the crescent rolls and place the long side up against the bottom of the bowl. Go around, touching the wide-end points of the crescent rolls. It should start to look like a starburst coming out from under the bowl. Then, go around again with the second can of rolls. The triangles should overlap.

Now, for the fun layering! Layer the mozzarella on the triangles up close to the bowl. Then, the pepperoncinis, basil, salami, ham, prosciutto, and provolone. Remove the bowl and bring the pointy part of the crescent roll over the top of the layers and pinch them to the wide part of the roll that was against the bowl. In between each point, some of the meat and cheese will peek through. Bake for 30 minutes. Slice it up and you have something that could also be called a pizza sandwich.

Listen to music together.

I recommend finding a good contemporary Christian radio station or stream it through your computer. If you have a grandchild who loves to dance or is musically inclined, this is an especially great way to be **together.** Rather than have the music in the background, truly listen to it and encourage your grandchild to express herself through motions or dance. Ask her about certain phrases and get her take on what it means in the song. It may not make sense to you, but it's good stuff going in her brain. After all, garbage in, garbage out…good stuff in, good stuff out. The key to this is if you're wanting to be **together,** YOU have to participate. Get past your inhibitions and dance!

Look through photos.

You have probably experienced how much your grandkids love seeing photos and videos of themselves. They're also intrigued to find out more about their parents. Spend some time **together** browsing old photo albums of when your son or daughter (one of their parents) was about their age. This activity can lead to some very interesting conversations.

They may notice that they look an awful lot like one of their parents. Insert just a sentence or two that makes them aware that even though God creates each of them to be unique, He also creates them as a mixture of their mom and dad. There may be familiar objects or background in some pictures. What stories do they cause to surface?

The younger the grandchild, the faster he will go through the photos. Older grandchildren may fixate on one photo that intrigues them and ask question upon question about it. Let the child lead the conversation with his inquiries. Although adults tend to be afraid of questions, for the most part, the questions lead to discoveries and very interesting opportunities to open up with your grandchildren.

Provide ribbon hugs.

My daughter-in-law did something very special for me when the twins were preschoolers and I was traveling a lot. She cut a piece of ribbon for each grandchild that was the length from right wrist to left wrist. Then she drew around their hands, cut them out, and glued them to each end of that grandchild's ribbon. A note was attached that said I should take the ribbons with me as I traveled. Anytime I felt a need for a grandma hug, I could wrap the ribbon around me. I carried those ribbons with me on many trips as a reminder that even though the miles separated us, we could still be **together.**

An heirloom you can pass on to your grandchildren is the assurance that you found great joy in spending time **together.**

"Watch"

"Watch this!" you hear your adventurous grandson yell as he stands at the end of the high dive board. "Grandma, are you watching?" your granddaughter asks with eyebrows raised as she gets ready to start her new gymnastics routine. After blowing the largest bubble of their lifetime and popping it all over their face, you hear, "Did you see that?" (Were you **watching**?)

As they get older, you don't hear the actual word **"watch"** like you did when they were little, but you see their eyes span the risers for you, to make sure your head isn't turned. They're checking to see if they are the center of your attention. When you're good at **watching**, your grandkids will invite you not only to games, but to rehearsals and practices.

> An heirloom you can pass on to your grandchildren is the assurance that you found great joy in spending time together.

One of your biggest jobs as a grandparent is to **watch**. Over and over again, you **watch** the same thing as your grandkids attempt to go further or get better on each of their attempts. They don't want you to miss the big one—the success! **Watch** with your entire body. Smile and nod to acknowledge their attempts. Clap like crazy when you can tell they are pleased with what they accomplished. (I'm known to let out a pretty rambunctious hoot and holler. I blame that on not being a very profound clapper.) "Yes, nailed it" or "You stuck the landing" are two of my grandkids' favorites to hear. Even though "stuck the landing" is a gymnastics term, it translates for us to be any time you followed through and got every bit of it right (whatever it might be).

*We have taken the grand-twins to a trampoline park twice a year for the past couple of years. It's amazing how their abilities change in just a few months. Fortunately, Grandma and Grandpa always go together. That way we can each take one kid and **watch** their amazing feats. It's so fun to be a **watching** cheerleader!*

Mom and Dad have full plates. They just can't do everything, and kids can never be **watched** as much as they want. **Watching** takes a lot of time, and you can't do it when you're doing something else. It calls for undivided attention. To be **watched** is a need in your grandchild that you can provide.

Why is **watching** important for you to do for your grandkids? It gives them a sense that you are always there for them. It's security. It makes them feel like they're the only one on the stage, because you're there to **watch** only them, not every other kid on the playground or the team. It sends them the emotional message that you not only can, but that you enjoy focusing your attention on just them. That emotional message will serve you well when it translates into them desiring to have a hard-topic, one-on-one conversation with someone. They'll gravitate to the person they know who will just sit back and **watch** as they share their questions and thoughts, who will focus on them and shut out the distractions of the world, who will cheer them on to follow God's leading.

Oh my, you get the privilege of **watching**. Don't take this responsibility lightly.

Name some opportunities you have to **watch** your grandkids.

1. _____

2. _____

3. _____

"With"

Whether you're the parent with only one or you have a houseful of kids, you just want to get through the next 24 hours. Being the grandparent is a different story most of the time. There is a luxury that grandparents have that parents don't. I'm not speaking for all grandparents, but most have less on their schedules than they have had in the past or are even retired. After all, their kids are grown and should be out of the house. No more figuring out when you could possibly have dinner because one kid has marching band practice, another has his first job, and another has a leadership club event—all for which you must act as chauffeur. The luxury I'm speaking of is the power of **with**. Most grandparents have the time to simply be **with** their grandkids. As grandparents, you get to notice the little things that you were too busy to take notice of when you were the parent in your house.

*I realized how special the word **with** is when Bowen and Kendall spent the night one weekend. Although they had plenty of bubble baths and fun things to do in the tub at home, many bath times were more like going through a carwash, especially after they started school. One parent announced it was time for a bath, the kids stripped down while the other parent ran the water, and then the kids were barely in the tub long enough to get completely wet when the towel awaited them. They are just like every ordinary family who needs to cram an awful lot into their evenings.*

*On the other hand, our evening plans as grandparents—all we had to get done, all that was on our to-do list—was "have kids over for the night." We didn't have anywhere we needed to be. There was nothing we had to do. All that awaited the kids was what they wanted to do for as long as they wanted to do it. It wasn't unusual for them to spend over an hour like little fish in the bathtub. I leaned against the cabinet and listened to the giggles coming from the tub as the two of them squirted each other and poured from one container to another. My assignment was simple. My mission was to be **with** them.*

My son and daughter-in-law are amazing parents, and they give all three kids an incredible amount of personal attention. But they need a break sometimes. It brings me great joy to know they can be confident that any of the grandparents are ready and willing to let them chill or just be kid-less for a bit, while knowing that the kids are getting quality **with** time.

This **with** thing really has very little to do with age. *I walked in their door the other day and Bowen couldn't get to me fast enough. Even though the house was full of people, he wanted to be **with** me. He wanted my attention…right then. I had my arms loaded with dishes for dinner, but dinner was totally invisible to Bowen. He wanted to tell me about the drone he ordered and just be **with** me. I was the only one in the house who had not heard the drone news. I tried to put him on pause so I could get my coat off, but he started telling me about the drone features before the second arm got out of the sleeve. I love **with** times when my grandkids know that they can ramble on and on as long as they want to.*

This kind of **with** desire doesn't happen overnight. It builds over time as you set things aside and communicate with your grandchild that you just want to be **with** him or her. Everything else is less important. Bowen is confident that I love to listen to his descriptions and stories…and he knew I was going to be just as excited about the drone as he was. (Truthfully, I couldn't wait for it to arrive, because if it did everything the manufacturers claimed it would, this was going to be awesome!)

I'm a super busy person. (I can hear my husband saying "amen" to that.) There was a time when I had a list of my different to-do lists. My grandkids have changed how I operate, though. I would rather let the stuff on my to-do list get pushed to another day than to pass up an opportunity for **with** time. I want them to remember me as a grandparent who would stop her world to be **with** them.

When would be good **with** times for you and your grandchildren?

1. _____

2. _____

3. _____

Let the Scriptures Speak

■ 1 Timothy 4:12 (NIrV)

Don't let anyone look down on you because you are young. Set an example for the believers in what you say and in how you live. Also set an example in how you love and in what you believe. Show the believers how to be pure.

I'm going to take some liberties with this verse and stretch our thinking a bit. This verse is intended to encourage young people to recognize that they are not too young to be an example to the body of Christ. They can model a life of following God as well as any believer. Just as young people shouldn't let others look down on them merely because of their age, I think older people need to be reminded of that also. They shouldn't think their worth to the body of Christ is less because of their number of years. So, don't let anyone look down on you because you are OLD!

There are lots of words to say and stories to tell. But, there's also a life to be lived—a life that is full-blown, all in, as a child of God. It's not reserved for the young. It is a life that your grandchildren need to see modeled right in front of their eyes. They need to see you reading your Bible. They need to see your commitment to your local body of believers. They need to see you **passionately** worshiping. They need to see how you handle the aches and pains that come with age. They need to see you sharing your faith with others. They need to see how you find new ways to serve in God's kingdom, since your energy level is not as strong as you age. They need to see that there is no expiration date on how long you can be an active, enthusiastic follower of Christ.

> ...Don't let anyone look down on you because you are old!

Your grandchildren, whether 2, 22, or 42, are listening and watching you. Model a life that pleases God. He wired our brains with around 30,000 fibers that carry auditory data, and fibers that carry visual data numbering over a million (according to Rock and Page in *Coaching with*

---

* Rock, David, and Linda J. Page, PhD. *Coaching with the Brain in Mind.* Hoboken, NJ: John Wiley & Sons, 2009.

the Brain in Mind*). That tells me something very important: We need more SHOW than TELL. Our stories are significant and need to be told, but our grandchildren want to see us depending on the faithfulness of God as we did in days gone by. The impact of living an authentic life of commitment to God will have an exponentially greater impression on your grandchildren than what you can recall to them—they want to be part of the rest of your story.

■ 3 John 1:4 (ESV)
I have no greater joy than to hear that my children are walking in the truth.

Take a moment and list the things that you'd like to see as part of your grandchild's life. What do you want for them? A loving spouse? An exciting career? A beautiful home? Good health? No problems? A college education? These are the things that would bring you joy if they made up your grandchild's life. We'll come back to your list in a moment.

I love the word "joy!" When I've been so fortunate to have that pure moment of joy, it's characterized by squeals of delight, chicken skin (or as some of you call them—goosebumps), eyes that well up about to overflow, a *needert* (a term my husband coined that describes how I twiddle all my fingers together right at my chin when I'm really tickled by something), and butterflies in my stomach. I admit, I'm a bit overly-expressive sometimes. That's how joy manifests itself for me, though. Now, what's yours? How do you express the joy you're experiencing? What do you do that makes you feel like you're smiling from head to toe?

Now, back to your list. Which one of the things you listed would bring you THE GREATEST joy? Which one would cause you to react with your special expression of joy? Did your grandchild's salvation and close daily walk with the Lord even make the original list? All the things I listed in the first paragraph would make me extremely happy if they were part of my grandchild's life. I would celebrate with them and support them relentlessly in those pursuits. But as I thought about it, none of those things would call forth squeals of delight, chicken skin, or a spontaneous *needert*. This I do know, though. On the day they profess their faith in Jesus Christ, I will go bonkers…berserk! The reason I know that is because that's how I react every time one of the kids in our children's ministry makes that commitment. And, the kids who are most precious to me—my grandkids—will undoubtedly receive that reaction…only on steroids.

There is NO GREATER joy than to know that my grand-kiddos are walking with THE Way, THE Truth, and THE Life. Seriously, my life will feel complete when that happens for each one of my precious charges. I can't wait to experience that joy…three times over. I think about it all the time. I pray every single day, relentlessly, that they will fall head-over-heels, passionately in love with the Jesus I have followed and sat at the feet of since I was 13.

John wrote this letter to one of his spiritual children, a man named Gaius who had probably come to salvation through the influence of John. John had seen many sorrows along the way, even witnessing the crucifixion of Jesus, and could've said that being free of those sorrows brought him the greatest joy. But he didn't. He recognized that knowing Gaius was walking in the Truth brought him the greatest joy in his life.

As you rank the things that bring you joy, move away from considering the things of this world, which is what our original list consisted of, and move toward the things your grandchildren will take with them into eternity. Focus your energies and your prayers to that end, knowing that it will bring you the greatest joy of your lifetime.

■ Deuteronomy 4:9–10 (NLT)

But watch out! Be careful never to forget what you yourself have seen. Do not let these memories escape from your mind as long as you live! And be sure to pass them on to your children and grandchildren. Never forget the day when you stood before the Lord your God at Mount Sinai, where he told me, "Summon the people before me, and I will personally instruct them. Then they will learn to fear me as long as they live, and they will teach their children to fear me also."

When the decades have mounted up, and they no longer bother to put the number of candles on your birthday cake that represent the years you have had breath (in fear of setting off a smoke detector), the lane called Memory Lane is more like a cross-country highway. Your collection of years just means that you have more memories. It means that God has coordinated more opportunities for you to find Him faithful.

These verses start out with a loud and clear exclamation of caution: *"Be careful never to forget…."* It may be tempting to think, "Oh, no one wants to hear about what happened to me years ago," but that's simply not the truth. Walk down Memory Lane often to affirm to yourself how God was faithful in all kinds of situations. (Just don't stay there.) When did you answer His call to be His child? Never forget that day. How did He make Himself known during an illness? Never forget that day. How did He renew your strength when you were a young parent raising kids and grasping for a full night's sleep? Never forget that day. When did He make it obvious that what happened wasn't just a coincidence, but it was His directed miracle? Never forget that day. When did He confirm the decision you had before you? Never forget that day. When did He break your heart because of someone's need, and when did He prompt you to be the one who could offer help? Never forget that day. Never let your special God-moment memories leave your mind.

> Your collection of years means... that God has coordinated more opportunities for you to find Him faithful.

As you recall each one, it will strengthen your faith, but God also intends so much more to come from those experiences. They were not for you alone. He says to pass them on to your children and grandchildren. He doesn't say it casually, though. He says to *be sure* (Deuteronomy 4:9, NLT) to pass them on to your children and grandchildren. This is your charge. This is your assignment. This is your mandate. This is a ministry God has given you *for such a time as this* (Esther 4:14, NLT).

When you surround yourself with your grandchildren, or as the verse says, *Summon the people before me* (Deuteronomy 4:10, NLT), God will instruct them. He will use the experiences you have had to instruct your grandchildren. The result will be that they, too, will desire to make God the center of their lives. They will see the life you have lived and want that for themselves. They will see how you leaned on the One True God for strength and direction and realize that it is the best way to do life.

So, take the hand of your grandchild and go for a walk, a walk down Memory Lane, a place where you found God faithful with each step.

■ **Genesis 48:9** (NLT)

"Yes," Joseph told him, "these are the sons God has given me here in Egypt."
And Jacob said, "Bring them closer to me, so I can bless them."

A wonderful thing you can do for your grandchildren is to bless them. A blessing can be prayed over them, written to them, or told to them in a special moment. What is a blessing, anyway? Good question. It sounds very religious, doesn't it? It's really much simpler than it sounds. It's merely a statement about your grandchild that communicates why they are so dear to you, why they bring you such joy, and how you see God working in their life both now and in the future. A blessing affirms those things and blankets your grandchild in positive, godly messages.

You don't bless your grandchild in private where they can't hear you. In the scripture quoted above, Jacob said to bring them close to him in order for him to bless them. He wanted to be able to touch them and speak over them. The mental picture I get of a blessing is embracing my grandchildren, and then handing them into God's protection. These simple, intentional, thought-out statements remind your grandchilden who they are in God's sight and in your sight.

So, what could a blessing include? By no means is this exhaustive, but it could be any assortment of answers to these questions.

- What makes you proud of your grandchildren?
- How do they make you feel when they are around?
- What spiritual gift(s) do you see God placing in their life?
- What do you pray for your grandchildren?
- What have you observed about the way they treat others?
- Why are you thankful that God paired you with your grandchildren?
- How have you seen these grandchildren grow?
- How is this grandchild unique from his/her siblings or other children in your life?
- Most importantly, remind them that they are created in God's image.

This should give you a better idea of what a blessing consists of and what it accomplishes. Bring your grandchildren close (even if it has to be through technology) and bless them.

My child, listen to me and do as I say,
and you will have a long, good life.
I will teach you wisdom's ways
and lead you in straight paths.

One of the best things any person can have is a relationship with an older, wiser believer who shares her or his life experiences with you. I hope that I'm not so stubborn, smug, or self-reliant that I think I have all the answers. I want to be sincerely glad when the stories I've been told keep me from making huge personal mistakes.

When you have frequent contact with your grandchildren and have built a healthy relationship with them, you have earned the right to share the wisdom God has given you. By absorbing your words and taking them to heart, hopefully your younger ones will draw on those experiences to avoid heartache and missed opportunities. You will lead them in straight paths.

I've read this scripture over and over, and the words that are seared in my mind are *"listen to me and you will have a long, good life."* Oh my,

> If I had ONE thing to say to my grandchildren.. ONE thing they would listen to... what would I say?

that's such an incredible responsibility to think that my words could lend themselves to someone else's long, good life. So, I've asked myself two questions: If I had ONE thing to say to my grandchildren…ONE thing they would listen to… what would I say? What do I consider a *"long, good life?"*

Let's start with the one thing I want them to listen to and believe as their own. This wasn't difficult for me to decide on, because I regularly share it with not only my grandchildren but with any children I have the blessing to lead. It's this: The most important decision you will ever make is the decision to follow or not to follow Christ.

That one decision will affect every other decision you will make in your entire life. It will affect who you choose as friends. It will affect the attitudes you have toward people in need. It will affect where you go to college and who you marry. It will affect the career you choose and what you do in your recreation time.

Now for the second question: What do I consider a *"long, good life?"* When you choose to follow Christ and make Him Lord of your life, you will have far fewer regrets over the actions you take. Why? Because you let God lead your life and He has wonderful plans for you that He's eager to share (Jeremiah 29:11). They are plans for a good life. If you're not following Him, you have not talked with Him about His plan, so there's no way to know His good and perfect gift. It's a wonderful thing to say that you accepted Jesus as your Savior at a young age and have followed Him all the days of your life.

A good life in the sight of God is when the Holy Spirit whispers into your heart, "Well done, my good and faithful servant." It has nothing to do with the amount of money you have, but it does have to do with how you steward that money. It has nothing to do with how many hours you spend at work, but it does have to do with how you use your time for the glory of God.

The long, good life comes about when you do what God created all people to do, and that is to bring Him glory through all our words and actions. This brings us to a third question: Is your life an example that your grandchildren *should* follow and imitate in order to have a long, good life? Are you living each day, each hour, each second with one thing in mind, which is to glorify the One who made you? Model it. Talk about it. Share your long, good life with your grandchildren in the hope that they will listen and take action. Consequently, they, too, will have the long, good life God has planned for them.

■ Psalm 26:7 (NIV)

[I go about] *proclaiming aloud your praise and telling of all your wonderful deeds.*

As Christians, we're really good at acknowledging God's handiwork during our times of prayer or using that opportunity to thank Him for all He created; however, in our day-to-day activities, we're not so quick to express our gratitude to our Almighty God.

It's important to praise God in the ordinary day-to-day events. Acknowledge His presence and power out loud.

■ Romans 1:11 (MSG)

I so want to be there to deliver God's gift in person and watch you grow stronger right before my eyes!

An enormous sadness sweeps over me when I think of grandparents who cannot live close to their grandchildren. Being able to hug my grandkids and have them in my home on a regular basis truly have been some of the happiest, most fulfilling parts of my life. We have been blessed beyond measure to have our employment situations be such that we could work from home…no matter where home might be. We also have only one child, so we jokingly tell him that he can run, but he can't hide from us!

Although Romans 1:11 isn't speaking specifically of grandparents and grandchildren, it does address that longing to be with someone, to watch them grow right before your eyes. If that isn't grandparenting, I don't know what is!

There are a few things I'd like to speak into concerning distance grandparenting. First of all, we live in a time where "right before my eyes" doesn't necessarily have to mean being in the same room physically. You can be in the same room through technology. If technology intimidates you, it's time you got over it! (I'm aware that may have sounded harsh, but it's for the sake of your grandchildren. I'm technologically-challenged, and I figure it out or ask for help. If I can do it, so can you!) My mother-in-law, who saw the twins for the first time via a Skype session, felt it was so real she reached out to rub their little faces on the screen. Technology has a beautiful way of eliminating distance. My daughter-in-law Facetimes her mother and sister multiple times each week. Consequently, all the grandchildren, whether in Georgia or Illinois, have an extremely close relationship with their grandparents. Don't miss out just because you're a little squeamish about technology.

What can you share when you Skype or Facetime? Read a book to your grandchild, stopping to hold the pictures up to the screen before turning the page. Or, let them read to you. Ask them to show you any art projects they may have done. Don't ask questions like, "How was school today?" or "What did you learn at school today?" Their answers to those questions will always be "nothing." Ask things like:

- Who's your best friend and what is she or he like?
- What was the best part of your day?
- What are you looking forward to doing?
- Tell me about your baseball game.

You want to ask questions that will start conversations and will get them talking, instead of you doing all the talking. Knowing that you will listen to them is a very strong and significant relationship builder.

The separation by miles brings another aspect of grandparenting to my mind. If you live in the Midwest and your grandchildren are on the West Coast, I'm sure you pray for them regularly—that someone will step into their lives to guide them and love them the way you would, up close and personal. Let me remind you that you're not the only one praying that prayer. There is a grandparent on the West Coast who is praying that someone in your Midwest town where their grandchild lives will guide and love their grandchild for them. There is a great opportunity for ministry here. Make note of kids who are in this situation and commit to be a surrogate grandparent. You could be the answer to a grandparent's prayer.

I'm sure your heart's desire is to be there in person to watch your grandchildren grow, but don't write off the possibilities that technology has to bring them close to you.

■ Ruth 4:13–15 (NASB)

So Boaz took Ruth, and she became his wife, and he went in to her. And the LORD enabled her to conceive, and she gave birth to a son. Then the women said to Naomi, "Blessed is the LORD who has not left you without a redeemer today, and may his name become famous in Israel. May he also be to you a restorer of life and a sustainer of your old age; for your daughter-in-law, who loves you and is better to you than seven sons, has given birth to him."

Keep in mind as you read these two Ruth passages that Naomi's son had been married to Ruth. He was killed in battle, along with his brother and Naomi's husband. Although Ruth was free to return to her people and had no obligation to Naomi, she chose to stay with her mother-in-law. Any children Ruth would give birth to would not be Naomi's grandchildren. Boaz is distantly related to Naomi, but it's a far stretch.

The son that this scripture speaks of is Obed, Boaz and Ruth's son, who would be the grandfather of David. It says, though, that this grandchild is a restorer of life and a sustainer of your old age! This child, who was not really Naomi's grandson, even though she treated him as such, had restored her life and given her purpose in her old age. In previous verses, the Scriptures share that people hardly recognized Naomi when she returned to her hometown. Life had been hard for Naomi, and her appearance showed it.

I know that I can be exhausted from the chores of my day, and then one of my grandkids shows up to run to me with open arms to be loved on, and I am restored. I'm given new life. Isn't that what grandkids do?

Ruth 4:16–17 (NASB)
Then Naomi took the child and laid him in her lap, and became his nurse. The neighbor women gave him a name, saying, "A son has been born to Naomi!"

Naomi stepped into the life of this infant who was not technically her grandchild. She must have loved Obed passionately, because the neighboring ladies described her as caring for him as if he were her own child. It sounds as though her neighbor friends were rejoicing with her as they witnessed the effect this baby had on a disheveled, depressed old woman.

There are children within your sphere of influence who live far from their natural grandparents, or for some reason their grandparents are not part of their lives. They're not even aware of how much they're missing. Have you ever thought of being a Naomi to a child you're not related to? What would it take for you to see a child who is not a blood-relation as your own?

> There are children who would love to have you as a grandparent.

Don't limit yourself to the traditional grandparent relationships. God blessed Naomi and gave her new life through baby Obed. There are children who would love to have you as a grandparent.

If a great distance separates you from your grandchildren, I'm sure it is your prayer that God provide someone in their life who will pour into them the way you would if you were actually there. More than likely, there is a child right under your feet (in your neighborhood or at church) whose grandparent is praying that same prayer from far away. You may be the person they are praying for, that God would prompt someone to step in and be a grandparent to their grandchild, pointing them to Jesus in everything they do.

We never assigned official grandparent names, like Mawmaw or Gramps. The twins came up with their own names when they were still giving one-word responses. They dubbed my husband, who is 6'5", Big Pa. And, my identifying title is Silly Grandma. When I started working in the children's ministry at the church where my son is the lead pastor, I couldn't figure out what the children should call me, since Bowen and Kendall were part of this group. Then, one of the kids asked, "Can we call you Silly Grandma?" I wasn't sure, because that is my special name from my grandkids. Bowen, Kendall, and I discussed it, and they were fine with other kids calling me Silly Grandma, as long as they asked Bowen and Kendall for permission first. So now, all new children get introduced to Silly Grandma with Bowen and Kendall's blessing. I share that with you, because all these kids see me as a very casual form of grandparent. I would never desire to take the place of their real grandparent, but the way they refer to me speaks volumes about our relationship. We are all part of the much bigger family—the family of God. The more grandchildren the better, as far as I'm concerned.

Are there children you could become a grandparent to? Kids who are missing out on a grandparent relationship?

1. _____

2. _____

3. _____

Scriptures to Memorize

I encourage you, for the sake of your grandparent-hood, to commit some specific verses to memory. I heard that! You doubt if the grey matter between your ears can handle Scripture memorization. Your brain may not do it as quickly as it used to, but yes, you can do this. And yes, you *should* do this!

These verses will give you confidence and hope when you're not sure of your place in your grandchild's spiritual development. Often, as I read scripture, it fills me with determination. God's voice inside me says, "You can do this. You can live out this scripture. You can point your precious grandkids to Jesus. Go get 'em!" God's Word applies to my life, and when it starts talking about "old age" and "gray hairs," I can totally relate!

There are 12 verses here, so it would be very easy to commit to memorize ONE verse each month. Keep reviewing the ones you learned as you add another to your collection. These words—God's words—will add to your identity as a grandparent. I guarantee it! As you go along, add other verses that speak to you in the role you play as a grandparent. Write them down and mark them in your Bible. They will make a heartwarming heirloom.

Psalm 71:18 (ESV)
So even to old age and gray hairs, O God, do not forsake me, until I proclaim your might to another generation, your power to all those to come.

Psalm 92:14 (NLT)
Even in old age they will still produce fruit; they will remain vital and green.

Judges 2:10 (NLT)
After that generation died, another generation grew up who did not acknowledge the LORD or remember the mighty things he had done for Israel.

Psalm 66:16 (NLT)
Come and listen, all you who fear God; and I will tell you what he did for me.

Malachi 4:4–6 (ESV)
Remember the law of my servant Moses, the statutes and rules that I com-

manded him at Horeb for all Israel. Behold, I will send you Elijah the proph-et before the great and awesome day of the LORD comes. And he will turn the hearts of fathers to their children and the hearts of children to their fathers, lest I come and strike the land with a decree of utter destruction.

3 John 1:4 (ESV)
I have no greater joy than to hear that my children are walking in the truth.

Psalm 145:4 (NLT)
Let each generation tell its children of your mighty acts; let them proclaim your power.

Deuteronomy 4:9–10 (NLT)
But watch out! Be careful never to forget what you yourself have seen. Do not let these memories escape from your mind as long as you live! And be sure to pass them on to your children and grandchildren. Never forget the day when you stood before the LORD your God at Mount Sinai, where he told me, "Summon the people before me, and I will personally instruct them. Then they will learn to fear me as long as they live, and they will teach their children to fear me also."

Joel 1:3 (NLT)
Tell your children about it in the years to come, and let your children tell their children. Pass the story down from generation to generation.

2 Timothy 3:14–15 (NLT)
But you must remain faithful to the things you have been taught. You know they are true, for you know you can trust those who taught you. You have been taught the holy scriptures from childhood, and they have given you the wisdom to receive the salvation that comes by trusting in Christ Jesus.

Isaiah 46:4 (NLT)
*I will be your God throughout your lifetime—
until your hair is white with age.
I made you, and I will care for you.
I will carry you along and save you.*

Proverbs 17:6 (NLT)
Grandchildren are the crowning glory of the aged; parents are the pride of their children.

Story Starters

You have entered the section of this book where you will be exploring ways to ease into a spiritual conversation with your grandchild. It probably hasn't crossed your mind to utilize objects around your house, or photographs, or a piece of clothing to tell your grandchild one piece of your faith story. To say that they need to hear your faith story is such an understatement. It can be a monumental factor in them making a decision to follow Christ.

At the end of each description of a Story Starter, you'll find a place to jot down your notes—what God has brought to your mind specifically about your story.

Most people assume the best way to have a spiritual conversation within the family is through devotions. While I highly recommend doing structured devotions with your grandchild, especially if they don't do them at home, these Story Starters will offer you many more possibilities. If you'd like to integrate structured devotions that are super fun to do together and engage everyone with scripture, check out two books my husband and I wrote called *Fun Family Devotions New Testament* and *Fun Family Devotions Old Testament*. These devotions are an adjunct resource to *Egermeier's Bible Story Book*.

Now…on to the rest of your story.

A Fascinating Object

Kids are fascinated by objects that don't normally appear in their everyday lives. The younger they are, the more wide-eyed they seem to be. But don't discount those teenagers and adult grandchildren. The uniqueness of the object draws them in and escorts them to a place where they want to know more. They want you to elaborate on what the significance of the object is.

When you present your grandchildren with a fascinating object—whether it's just sitting on a shelf, falls out when you open a cabinet, or something you intentionally bring out to show them—they naturally will have questions. The questions flow because they don't know much about the object. It fascinates them!

Although you'll most likely be sharing lots of memories that relate to the object, focus in on one spiritual lesson this object reminds you of. Use it to tell one specific thing God taught you.

To illustrate the point from my own life, there are two large trophies sitting on top of filing cabinets in our basement. Hanging from each trophy is a crown— one made of beads that look like pearls and the other covered in rhinestones. They're glamorous and sparkly...every little girl's dream. How can I use these crowns and trophies, which represent everything material and self-focused, to launch a spiritual conversation? The contrast between what they commonly represent and how God wants us to live is a perfect starting place.

I was an all-American girl—a Christian teenager, valedictorian of my graduating class, popular among my peers, disciplined in holding down a part-time job, played the piano and organ in my home church, and was crowned both Floyd County's Junior Miss and the Harvest Homecoming Queen. It seemed that everything I attempted to do was attainable. Then, on my 18th birthday, the reality of life hit me and hit me hard. I was diagnosed with crippling rheumatoid arthritis. Within three months of my diagnosis, I was unable to care for myself.

Those crowns and trophies represented all MY plans. They represented the direction I had for my life. Even though I was a committed Christian teenager, I never considered that God might have a plan different than mine. I never considered that God's plan might encompass something that wasn't easily attainable—something that might be difficult. Those objects represented my mistaken self-sufficiency.

But they also reminded me that I was a princess—not a princess in this world's meaning, but a princess for eternity—for I was a daughter of the King of heaven. I am the sister to the Prince of Peace. I belong to the royal family of God. My identity is not in the physical beauty that this world admires, but in the soul beauty that God welcomes into His family. It's more important to receive the crown that is waiting for me in heaven.

2 Timothy 4:8 (NIrV)
Now there is a crown waiting for me. It is given to those who are right with God. The Lord, who judges fairly, will give it to me on the day he returns. He will not give it only to me. He will also give it to all those who are longing for him to return.

It's important for me to tell my grandchildren that they, too, can receive a crown on the day Jesus returns if they have claimed Him as their personal Savior. Psalm 78:6 (NASB) says, *That the generation to come might know, even the children yet to be born, That they may arise and tell them to their children.* They won't know unless we tell them (Romans 10:14–15). Your faith stories and lessons are a wonderful tool God will use to lead your grandchildren in His direction.

What fascinating object could you use to tell your spiritual story?

1. _____

2. _____

A Photograph

Many people set a goal for their retirement to organize all the photos they've taken through the years. Although we all love looking at photos and remembering the special times they represent, those precious mementos are often stuffed into shoeboxes and spill out of grocery sacks.

You can't complete this enormous task in one day, so why not set up a card table in the corner of the den (a well-traveled place in your house) and chip away at organizing the photos? Anyone who comes in the house will notice the piles of pictures and be drawn to them, including your grandchildren. As they flip through the photos, you will have opportunity after opportunity to share stories, and it's the perfect time to share stories that impacted your spiritual journey. This is one of the most natural ways to step into sharing your story.

- What did that person in this picture say or do that helped you make a decision to follow Christ?

- How did that person help form the way you act or react?

- How was your life changed because they were part of it?

I have a special picture of Jackie Bryan, a lady in the church where we served in Garden Grove, California, when we were first married. The picture shows Jackie and another woman preparing a meal to take to someone who was recovering from surgery. That was so typical of Jackie. Even though she was a rather well-to-do woman, she had the heart of a servant and was a tremendous prayer warrior. But, as soon as I see this picture, the very first thing that comes to mind is something Jackie did that changed my life.

One Sunday Jackie approached my husband to invite us to be their guests at the Los Angeles County Fair that coming Friday night. It sounded like such fun, but Ray knew that walking was totally out of the question for me. At the time, I was very sick, and my goal for each day was being able to clean one room of our apartment. He declined the invitation, but Jackie negotiated that if I didn't feel like the fair, then they would take us out for a prime rib dinner. (That also sounded like great fun to my husband!)

Friday came, and I was having the best day I had experienced in months! Jackie and her husband took us out to a wonderful early dinner, then asked how we felt about trying the fair. I looked at Ray, and my eyes lit up. I wanted to go. So, off to the fair we went to take in as much as my body would allow. Larry, Jackie's husband, fed me rolls of dimes to toss at the plates and fish bowls to try to win a stuffed animal. I didn't win anything, but I had the time of my life trying! It was an absolutely wonderful evening and one that was pretty much free of pain. (I will admit that the next day I paid for my adventures, but it was so worth it.) Ray and I were both amazed at how I was able to enjoy all the activity of the fair that night.

On Sunday morning, Ray again thanked Jackie for the special night and expressed his amazement at how well I felt that night. Under her breath, Jackie muttered, "I knew she would." Ray asked her to repeat herself, and she said again, "I knew she would." Ray challenged how she would know such a thing. That's when Jackie revealed what she had done all week. After her initial invitation, Jackie decided that she would fast and pray ALL WEEK for me to have ONE pain-free night to enjoy the fair. She had gone without food all week…not asking for my healing, which is what so many other people had done, but to simply ask God to grant me one evening of relief and smiles.

When was the last time that you or I have fasted for an entire week on behalf of a friend, asking God for just one good night or one good afternoon? Jackie taught me so much about how to love a friend. She taught me so much about what it means to selflessly pray and fast for someone. What a beautiful memory that is! And so, the very first thing that comes to mind when I see her photo is how she fasted and stayed on her knees for me for a week.

I want my grandchildren to know about Jackie Bryan. She was a significant person in my life. Flipping through old photographs can provide the opportunity to share the story of how Jackie went to battle for me through prayer and how her life intersected mine.

What do you want your grandchildren's first thought of you to be when they go through their photographs after you have gone on to heaven? What kind of person do you want to be to them? When my three grand-kiddos see a picture of me, I want their first thought to be, "Silly Grandma loved Jesus and wanted to serve Him every breathing moment."

Describe 3 pictures you have that could start a spiritual conversation with your grandchild.

1. _____

2. _____

3. _____

A Phrase

We all have pet phrases we use—sometimes for a lifetime—sometimes just for a phase or season. They frequently are something said by mistake or a comment made to a silly situation. These phrases find themselves in conversations again and again in the coming months…or years.

For over a year, at one point in our marriage, we weren't sure where we were going to live and for how long. We had left our beautiful home in Hanford, California, and moved back to southern Indiana to live on my parents' farm. All our possessions were in boxes and stored in the barn. Our clothes were pretty much all that got unpacked that year. Often, we were looking for something that couldn't be found. Then someone would ask, "Do you know where the _____ is?" and the standard reply was, "It's PACKED AWAY!" It became part of our everyday language, because it was used exactly, word-for-word and with the same inflection, every single time. You didn't just say those words casually, you had to slowly and dramatically say them (complete with hands being raised to the sky) and finish it off with a heavy sigh.

"It's PACKED AWAY" became a phrase that reminded us of what we were going through. We were nomads waiting for our next assignment from the Lord. We had a fully furnished place to live, and there was no reason for us to want more. God had provided everything we needed for our time of transition (and uncertainty). Anytime we wanted something that was "packed away," it was merely for our additional pleasure, not a life-threatening need. God had provided for us during this uncertain time. If we went through the rest of our lives saying, "It's packed away," it was okay.

Do you see the spiritual impact that phrase could have when just a little more is told than the actual facts of the story? If that phrase comes up in a conversation—maybe the kids overhear us say it and laugh—it would be easy to just explain where it came from. But there's a bigger opportunity here. There's an opportunity to step into the story and share its spiritual implications. There's an opportunity to teach our grandkids that God provides what we need and that the material things we have are not as important as we sometimes think they are. It's the opportunity to say, "I believe it, because I've lived it." That's what sharing your spiritual stories comes down to.

Start looking for those connections that relate to your family's funny phrases, and don't fail to share the spiritual lessons they teach.

What phrases have been used in your family that could help you share a spiritual truth?

1. _____

2. _____

3. _____

Clothing

A piece of clothing can be a smooth conversation starter. More than likely you have kept a prom dress, a jersey, a jacket, or some crazy patterned socks because there's a back story—a memory attached to it. It commemorates an important time or event in your life. That back story has a special meaning to you. Are any of those stories connected with God's story in your spiritual journey?

Little girls, especially, love to play dress-up, and clothing can be a great jumping off point to tell part of your faith story. My granddaughter and I were in the basement when she noticed a piece of clothing covered in a dry-cleaning bag, barely touching the floor from where it hung amid the open rack of costumes. When she asked, "What's in the bag?" I pulled the plastic wrap away without hesitation to reveal a glimpse of a beautiful blue formal gown with sparkles covering the bodice. Her eyes lit up. What little girl doesn't like a princess dress!

"Whose is this?" That question told me she was ready to hear a story, so I stepped into the moment.

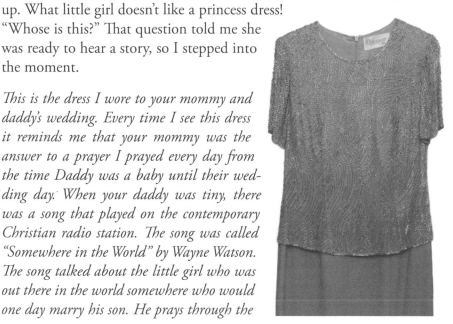

This is the dress I wore to your mommy and daddy's wedding. Every time I see this dress it reminds me that your mommy was the answer to a prayer I prayed every day from the time Daddy was a baby until their wedding day. When your daddy was tiny, there was a song that played on the contemporary Christian radio station. The song was called "Somewhere in the World" by Wayne Watson. The song talked about the little girl who was out there in the world somewhere who would one day marry his son. He prays through the

music that she will grow to love Jesus and hold on to Him.

I decided to start praying for the little girl who would one day marry my son, Jarad. I didn't even know her name, but I found out years later that her name was Kelley. I prayed for her mommy and daddy to be the very best parents… and that's your Ridenour Grandma and Silly Pa. This dress reminds me of how I prayed every day for the little girl I didn't know, but who has become a treasure in my life—your mommy. God listened to my prayer every day and prepared your mommy and daddy to love each other as they live for Him.

I was extremely ill when our son was little, and I never dreamed I'd live to share his wedding day. This beautiful gown marked a day when I recognized God's faithfulness at walking through so much with our family. Jarad is a godly man, pursuing the ministry, honoring both his parents and his God.

My husband has a football jersey from the days when he was part of the Booster Club at Anderson College. The only time we see the jersey is when we stumble across it during a move. At that time, Boosters were known for being followers of Christ, and many of the members were preparing for ministry. There's an entire book of stories triggered by this jersey that my husband could tell. This worn out, musty-smelling piece of sports clothing could be the conversation starter for sharing how Grandpa grew in Christ through those college years. Many of those Boosters are lifelong friends and still hold one another accountable these many years later. I'm sure the football jersey will someday help tell the story of how God worked in Big Pa's life.

What clothes do you have that could be connected to your spiritual story? Is it a costume worn in a play, a birthday party dress, the suit you were ordained in?

1. _____

2. _____

3. _____

Furniture

Many times, significant faith decisions have been made while physically positioned at a specific piece of furniture. It may have been while sitting around the kitchen table with the entire family. It may have been while lying on your back in the middle of your bed, staring up at the spots on the ceiling. Or perhaps, it was beside that same bed as you knelt in prayer. Do you have a spiritual experience connected with a porch swing at the summer camp lodge? Or a dilapidated unsteady stool where you watched your grandpa tinker at his tool bench? Or how about a rocking chair?

One of my most significant spiritual experiences happened in a rocking chair. We had purchased this particular big stuffed rocker for those middle-of-the-night feedings for our infant son. I actually tried it out to make sure I could rock easily, hold him, and stay half-asleep while getting plenty of support but not stretching my arms too far. It was the most comfortable—and most comforting—chair I've ever sat in.

After my diagnosis of rheumatoid arthritis, the disease spread quickly, and within a few months I was experiencing unceasing, excruciating pain which resulted in an inability to take care of many of my personal needs the way I was used to doing, much less, to do the things I had always enjoyed. One of those things was playing the piano and organ. I gave my first recital at the age of five, and as a young teenager, I was a regular on the instrument rotation at my home church. Now, I couldn't play. My fingers would hardly move and definitely couldn't stretch to create the sounds of an octave.

As I prayed for healing, I bargained with God that if He would heal me, I would play the piano and organ like He had never heard before. (Can you imagine? I was proposing to God that I could play music more beautifully than He had ever created. I shake my head now at how arrogant I must've sounded to Him.) I promised to devote my life to using those abilities to help people praise Him. That wasn't some fantasy promise; I really meant every word of it. My mistake, though, was in my understanding of prayer. Although I could mouth the words that said I believed God answered prayer by saying, "Yes," "No," or "Wait," what I really believed was that God answered, "yes" or "wait until I say yes." For over 10 years I put my life on hold, waiting for God to heal me…yes, so I could serve Him better.

Around 3:00 a.m. one night, the pain was especially overwhelming, and I pulled myself from bed to go sit in "the" rocking chair. I didn't want to wake my husband with the sobbing that came occasionally with the pain, so I retreated to the comfy chair. The gentle rocking seemed to calm me down. Nestled in the cushions and swaying back and forth, I found myself crying out to God for an answer. This time it was different. "God, I want so badly to be healed and be able to play the piano again for You. But I don't think I can go on living in this limbo of waiting to be healed. I need a yes or a no. And, whatever Your answer is, please give me the strength to live with it."

It was my spiritual tipping point. It was the place God wanted me to get to, and He was willing to wait 10 years to hear those words. Immediately, I felt His voice echo throughout my body. It was not an audible voice, and yet it was so real the words felt like they soaked into me. "I love you, Tina, but I'm not going to heal you. I know this leaves a hole in you, but I promise to fill that hole if You let me. I promise to fill that hole with My joy, if you will claim it each day." You may think that my reaction was one of insurmountable disappointment, but it was just the opposite. I was so grateful to have an answer, so grateful to be able to move on with my life, so grateful to pick up my life and move out of the Land of Wait. The tears I had been crying that night now changed from drips of desperation to streams of relief.

The next morning, my husband greeted me in the kitchen. When he looked at me, his face was questioning what he saw. "You look different. Did something happen?" I said, "Yes, we need to talk. God told me last night that I'm not going to be healed…and it's okay."

My grandkids need to know that story. They've watched Silly Grandma cope with the physical struggles every day of their lives. They need to know that God still speaks to people. It's not just a Bible story thing. They need to know that God answers prayer in three profound ways, and one of those ways is *no*. To be one of His mature followers, you need to accept the no answers as readily as the yes answers. My grandchildren need to know that there's no reason to be afraid of God's no answer. And that conversation can start with a piece of furniture—a rocking chair that acts as a bridge to help my grandkids understand the nature of God and the response of His followers.

Look around your house and think about the stories that are associated with pieces of furniture. When you're sitting with your grandchildren, watching a TV show, and the commercial comes on, you can hit the mute button and tell them the story behind the piece of furniture they are sitting on or that's always been present in that room. Snatch that moment to share one piece of your spiritual story. It will only take as long as a commercial, and, if it goes longer, be thankful that what you're sharing with them is more important than the show that's coming back on.

What piece of furniture has a spiritual story attached to it?

1. _____

2. _____

3. _____

A Shared Experience

One of the best ways to build any relationship is to work alongside one another on a project. The project itself provides a point of conversation. As you work on something together, questions arise, problems need to be solved, and an abundance of "I wonder what would happen if you did it a different way" conversations emerge. (Kids are especially good at that wondering part.) Just like any conversation, one thing leads to another, and you end up talking about all kinds of things.

One of the things that is especially appealing to kids when it comes to working on a project together is that the job doesn't feel like as much of a chore. It doesn't feel like work when you're sharing the task with someone else, when you're not carrying the entire load.

Depending on what part of the country you live in, there is some sort of U-Pick farm for the area's fruits or vegetables. It could be blueberries in northern Indiana and Michigan, peaches in Georgia, or strawberries in California. Visiting a U-Pick farm with your grandchild, no matter their age, is a great experience to share.

As you bend over to pick or climb a ladder to fill a basket, it's the perfect time to talk about growing. Introduce an "I wonder" thought: *I wonder what all the steps are that a farmer has to go through to get this crop ready for us to pick. I've driven past here several times the last couple of months, and it never looks the same.* Educate your grandchild on some unique information that you know about this particular crop. *I knew this field was table grapes or wine grapes, but it most definitely wasn't grapes for raisins. The rows of table grapes and wine grapes go north and south. The rows of grapes used for raisins go east and west. That's because they lay the grapes out on the ground on big pieces of paper to dry in the sun. If the vines are going east and west, the sun is on them all day long and they dry much faster and more evenly.*

In the flow of your interesting conversation about how this fruit or vegetable grows, you can transition very easily into talking about how they are growing. Kids absolutely love to hear stories (and see pictures on your phone) of when they were younger and doing things they now consider silly. This is the perfect time to brag on how you have seen them grow—physically, socially, emotionally, and intellectually. To hear those words of affirmation come out of your mouth raises the "endearment gauge." You just became more valued in their sight.

But, don't stop there! Where does God fit into this idea of growing? *You know, that farmer had a plan for what he had to do for that little strawberry seedling to produce these great big juicy red strawberries. He didn't put the plant in the ground and walk away. No, he had a plan for when the rows needed to be fertilized, when they needed to be weeded, and how much water they needed to receive. God has a plan for you, too, kiddo. He knows what you have been designed to do. He knows what you'll have to go through in order to serve Him best. He knows the mistakes you're going to make and the things you're going to be successful at. And, God wants you to rely on Him every day, every moment of your life, so that His plan for you will happen.*

What experiences can you plan to share with your grandchild? Even though God may lead the conversation in a different direction, what spiritual conversation could be part of your experience?

1. _____

2. _____

3. _____

A Significant Place

There are special places that I drive by, or simply think of the setting, and it prompts me to recall something significant that happened there. It would be so easy to talk about a significant place with your grandkids by starting the story with, "That's where…."

- That's where your grandpa asked me to marry him.

- That's where I made my decision to follow Christ and accept His salvation.

- That's where God confirmed that He was calling me to serve Him as a pastor (or whatever God has called you to).

- That's where I attended my first Bible study.

- That's where I sat for a couple of hours talking with my friend when her mother died.

- That's where I got away during college to think and pray.

- That's where I was baptized.

When I was 13, our youth group at my home church in New Albany, Indiana, went to a youth rally in Bedford. I didn't normally ask friends to go with me to youth outings, but on this day, I had asked my boyfriend to go along. At the end of the main service, the speaker asked if anyone wanted to make a personal decision to admit their sin to God and ask for His forgiveness. That's what I wanted more than anything, but I hesitated to go forward. Why? Embarrassingly, I have to say it was because I didn't know what my boyfriend would think. A close friend in the youth group, George, could see the struggle in my body language. He confronted me with my lack of decision-making before we left the rally. We decided that at church the next day, among the people who were my spiritual family and who understood salvation, I would make that public decision.

Sunday morning the pastor gave an invitation at the end of the service, and my feet stuck to the floor. I heard steps coming down the pew and then felt a hand grab mine. It was George. His little bit of a tug was enough to get my body to move and walk to the front of the church with him. These two places—the rally in Bedford and the morning worship service in New Albany— are places I identify where I made the most important decision of my life.

To see Bedford, Indiana, on the map, on a road sign, or to drive through the town, is an immediate association with my salvation experience. That's where I surrendered to Jesus.

Your sharing may start when you have the grandkids in your car and you drive past a significant place. It may be that you have a photo of the place displayed in your home. If so, consider adding a caption to it that teases and causes them to ask you a question about its significance, something such as, "New life began here."

It could also be a great story starter if you don't normally have the picture hung. Get it out, frame it, and place it in a conspicuous place. It'll be obvious that something is different, and your grandkids are likely to ask, "Where's this?"

List 3 significant places that would finish this sentence for you.

1. That's where _____.

2. That's where _____.

3. That's where _____.

 *Snack*

"Who wants a snack?" I think on possibly one occasion the reply was "Not me." Every other time, the answer has been an enthusiastic "I DO!" Since it appears that all kids like snacks, whether they're 2 years old or 18 years old, it would be smart for grandparents to figure out how they can use the goodness of a snack to launch a spiritual conversation.

Full disclosure: I've written a book called *More Than Cookies and Punch*, which includes about 50 different snacks. It not only tells you how you can make these snacks along with your grandchildren, but it also gives you questions to ask that will gracefully lead you to the Bible. Now that's a great combo! (Commercial over.)

One of the keys to using a snack as a story starter is to make it together. Many times, the launching point comes as the ingredients are assembled. One of my favorites is called "The Fourth Marshmallow."

The Goodies You'll Need:
• Whole graham crackers

• 4 large marshmallows for each graham cracker

• Large cookie sheet

• Oven

King Nebuchadnezzar had a 90-foot-tall gold statue made for the people to worship. The law was made that when the music played, everyone would have to bow down and worship the idol. Those who failed to obey would be thrown into the fiery furnace. When the music played everyone bowed down except Shadrach, Meshach, and Abednego. They refused to worship anything other than God. When someone reported Shadrach, Meshach, and Abednego to the king, he gave them one last chance to bow down when the music played, but still they refused.

The three men told the king that even if God did not save them from the furnace, they would not bow down and worship an idol. Shadrach, Meshach, and Abednego were tied up and thrown into the furnace. The furnace was so hot that the flames jumped out and killed the soldiers who threw the men in. But, when the king looked in the furnace, he saw four men, not three, walking around, and one of them looked like the Son of God. The king had the men pulled from the furnace, and they didn't even have the smell of smoke in their clothes! Surely, they served a mighty God! The king changed the law so that everyone had to worship the God of Shadrach, Meshach, and Abednego.

The Fun Stuff

Have each grandchild place a whole graham cracker on the cookie sheet.

Each grandchild will place one marshmallow on the graham cracker and identify it as Shadrach.

Add another marshmallow and identify it as Meshach. And another for Abednego. There are now 3 marshmallows on each graham cracker.

Carry the cookie sheet to the oven, preheated to 350°, and place it inside.

Immediately, tell the grandchildren to use this time while the marshmallows cook to go wash their hands.

As soon as they leave, add a marshmallow to each of the graham crackers.

When the grandchildren return, they will look inside the oven door and count the marshmallows on their graham cracker. Now there are four!

Whatcha' Think?

- How many men were thrown in the furnace?

- What surprised King Nebuchadnezzar when he looked in the furnace?

- What did Shadrach, Meshach, and Abednego tell the king when he tried to give them a second chance?

Shadrach, Meshach, and Abednego told King Nebuchadnezzar that even if God did not save them from the furnace that they would still serve Him. **Now, step in!** This is your chance to tell your grandchildren about a time when you prayed for something and it didn't happen. Share with them that your mind and heart were the same way as you prayed, "I will continue to serve You, God, even if You don't choose to answer my prayer the way I've asked."

What a fun, yummy, and on point way to serve up part of your faith story to your grandkids…of any age.

I could use these snacks to share my faith story.

1. _____

2. _____

3. _____

A Special Bible

We are truly blessed in the United States to have access to personal Bibles. Many of us, in fact, have several Bibles, each one serving a unique purpose. There are study Bibles that give you all the additional interesting cultural facts, family heritage Bibles where you can record information about generations, Bibles with devotionals that challenge you to personalize the scriptures you just read, and so, so many more.

Do you have a special Bible that you use on a regular basis? Or one that has a personal purpose?

Scripture memorization is a very important holy habit to me. For a long time, I didn't think I had time to add Scripture memorization to my already super busy schedule. But I found that there were times throughout my day that I could reclaim and use to store away God's Word in my heart and mind. I have a bunch of different methods and techniques that I utilize to master the short verses and the long passages: (I've written an entire book called *Hiding the Word* that shares lots of ideas on the topic.) For several years I worked for a sub-company of Awana, and it is required of all Awana employees that they memorize scripture. Employees are held accountable to meet that requirement. That gave me an additional incentive to incorporate Scripture memorization into my daily routine. I also love using the music of Seeds and JumpStart3 to memorize scripture to song. I may not be able to say the scriptures, but I can sing them!

The number of scriptures I had committed to memory were mounting, and I wanted a way that I could visually keep tabs on what I had accomplished. So, I pulled out a Bible that was otherwise untouched and started highlighting in bright pink the verses I knew by heart. I always make notes in any Bible I'm reading, but this particular Bible is devoted entirely to recording my Scripture memorization. There are no comments in the margins, no verses underlined in pen, and no verse references added next to any of the text. Only pink highlights. This particular Bible came in a wraparound snapping box, and it has a perfect place for keeping the highlighter handy.

I have a shelf in my home office that is filled with Bibles. The twins were having a great time thumbing through them, especially looking for ones that had interesting artwork depicting the stories. They had some questions about each Bible—about comments that were in special boxes, lists, and diagrams. Then, they opened the box which contained my Scripture memorization Bible. Their first question was why this Bible had its own box. I really had no answer but told them it was to hold the pink marker.

As they flipped through this Bible, they saw some lines in pink on this page, and then another couple of lines in pink a few pages later. For a six-year-old, any time they see markings in a book, they're trying to figure out if someone is in trouble, or if it's okay in this situation. They sure didn't want to get blamed for making the pink marks in Silly Grandma's Bible!

I explained what the significance was of each pink highlighted verse—that I was tracking the scriptures I had memorized. This led to my opportunity to share with them how important it is for followers of God to memorize His Word. The Bible is God's message to us, and we don't ever want to be without it. Who knows? We could be in a situation one day when the government we live under doesn't allow us to have a Bible. If that happens, they can't take away what we have in our heads and hearts.

Being able to explain the reason for this Bible demonstrated to my grandkids that Silly Grandma was still actively changing, that I am still actively pursuing ways that I can get closer to my Savior and Lord. It is so important for your grandkids to see that your faith is much more than a Sunday morning Bible story, and that Scripture memorization is for all believers, not just kids.

You may not have a Scripture memorization Bible but placing the Bible you use for your daily devotions out where your grandkids can see it is a wonderful statement that your faith is part of your everyday life. Let them see you open your Bible, even if they are not part of the reading or discussion. The message they will receive is that you set aside a portion of each day to have time alone with God and His Word.

I would encourage you to share with your grandkids how you are pursuing an active, growing faith and not just share what has happened in the past.

How can you use a Bible to start a spiritual conversation with your grandchild?

1. _____

2. _____

3. _____

A Year with a Bible

This item is a little different from all the others I've included in this section. Rather than looking back on your life and finding ways to tell the story God has written on your life, you are looking forward to the story that God will write on your grandchild's life. This can be done no matter the age of your grandchild.

Choose one grandchild and purchase a new Bible that will fit him or her best. There are lots of different styles of Bibles with various helps. This is a Bible for a lifetime, so avoid ones that are directed specifically at children. It needs to have wide margins and lots of white space, because you'll need space for what you'll be adding.

This project is best to start on January 1 of any given year. Commit to reading through the Bible you have purchased for your grandchild during that coming year. As you read, keep him or her in mind. When single scriptures or entire passages speak to you, especially pertaining to him, underline or highlight that scripture. Then write the Scripture reference in the margin, along with the thoughts you had about her and the scripture.

If you're thinking right now that you don't have a clue as to what you should write, let me give you a few examples. Here are some passages that jump out at me when I think of my grandkids.

Highlight Jeremiah 29:11 (NLT) – *"For I know the plans I have for you," says the Lord. "They are plans for good and not for disaster, to give you a future and a hope."*

The comment in the margin might be: *God has a plan for you, _____ (their name). And, it's a wonderful plan. I can't wait to see how He is going to use you in His kingdom. Your future is bright if you first give yourself completely to His plan.*

Highlight Isaiah 40:31 (NLT) – *Those who trust in the Lord will renew their strength. They will soar high on wings like eagles. They will run and not get weary. They will walk and not faint.*

The comment in the margin might be: *There have been times when I've felt weary and wanted to give up. This verse came to mind and it gave me new assurance that what I was going through was temporary and that God was the God of Restoration. There was light at the end of my tunnel. Many times, when I wake in the middle of the night before I even open my eyes, the words of this scripture are audibly coming from my mouth. I'm praying right now that you will always turn to the God of Restoration when you're feeling defeated, tired, or weary.*

Highlight John 1:12 (NLT). *But to all who believed him and accepted him, he gave the right to become children of God.*

The comment might be something like: *I look forward to the day when you confess your past to the Lord and claim Jesus as your Savior and Lord. I pray for that day and know that it will be one of the happiest days of my life. On that day, our relationship will change. You will no longer be just my grandchild, but more importantly you will be my sister/brother in the family of God. There will only be God and His children…no grandchildren and generations to follow.*

So, do you see why you need to choose a Bible with lots of room to write? Make sure you have not limited your ability to share your heart by choosing a Bible that has small margins.

In the front of many Bibles there is space to write *To* and *From*. Consider including a note on this page to express why you spent the year pouring over the scriptures in this particular Bible. And don't forget to date it. They'll be glad you did!

What 3 scriptures immediately come to mind that you'd like to highlight in a Bible for your grandchild?

1. _____

2. _____

3. _____

An Heirloom

Around the house and packed away are things that I've collected over the years. Many of them are little gifts that special people in my life have given me. Some of them need to be thrown in the trash because they've rotted or have turned yellow with age. Then, there are others that are nice, and even expensive gifts.

As with me, a part of your spiritual story may be attached to some of your gifts. Those items may have been given to you by someone you admired for her walk with the Lord, by someone who encouraged you in a challenging time in your life, or by someone who mentored you. It may have been a camp counselor who gave each one of his campers a gift as they left camp. It may be a souvenir that someone brought back for you from a special trip. The item or souvenir meant so much because of the person it came from.

Depending on what the item is, choose a time to present it to your grandchild, along with the spiritually impactful story that accompanies it. If it's something breakable or small that could slip through his or her hands or be easily misplaced, then wait until you're sure the grandchild will take proper care of it. Once it's in her or his care, revisit the story whenever that item comes out from where it's stored.

There was a precious godly woman in the church we served in Hanford, California, who was known for being a prayer warrior. Her name was Naomi Pfander. Naomi had a special chair in her home where she read her Bible and prayed diligently. She and her husband both worked for the school system all their adult lives, and when they retired, they knew that God was not finished with them. They felt God calling them to use those same gifts and talents they had used in public schools for decades in a new capacity on the mission field in Turkey. Naomi was the kind of Christ-follower I aspired to be. I want to be a prayer warrior and someone who never stops serving my Savior and Lord.

For some unknown reason, Naomi gave me a gift one day. There may have been a reason, but I'm sorry to say that I can't remember it. The gift was a beautiful china tea cup. I don't drink coffee, and I'm not a big tea drinker either, but that really didn't matter. This gorgeous tea cup was from Naomi. The cup sat in the display window of our china cabinet for many years or out on a shelf. Each time I noticed the cup, I referred to it in my mind as my "prayer cup." After all, it was from Naomi, the woman who had prayed for me repeatedly. I'll not know the extent of her prayers until I get to heaven. What I do know is that she prayed from that special chair on my behalf many times.

My granddaughter, Kendall, had a Christmas tea party and invited me to attend. Something struck me as I was getting ready to go, and I thought it was time to give Kendall this special tea cup. Although the cup was a treasure to me, it was time to share the story of Naomi. It was an opportunity to share with Kendall what a prayer warrior is.

I was the first to arrive at the tea party, and Kendall answered the door. She took my coat, and then I handed her the gift bag. She smiled and placed it under the tree. I told her it was a hostess gift for the hostess of the tea party, and she should open it right then. She was very excited to get a Christmas gift way before Christmas. When she pulled the cup from the wrapping, her eyes got wide and she said to her mother, "Oh look! Isn't it beautiful?" She handled it so gently. Then, she asked if she could replace her cup already on the table with her new china cup.

There was plenty of time before the other guests arrived, so I spent the next few minutes introducing Kendall to Naomi. I hope she always refers to the china cup as her grandma's "prayer cup." I hope she knows that the desire of her grandma's heart is to be a prayer warrior like Naomi. And the tea cup will be the occasional reminder of that.

What heirloom do you possess that has a spiritual story that goes along with it? Are you so attached to your heirlooms you can't part with them, even if their spiritual story will impact the life of your grandchild? You don't want to load your grandchildren down with things that you treasured, but two or three gifts of this kind as they grow up will not only share part of your spiritual story but will add to their own personal spiritual story.

One day, I'd like to give my grandchild _____,
and tell him or her about _____.

Hobby

Most people have a hobby—a way they escape the demands of everyday life and go to a place where they can learn about a specific subject or create something that is from their own imagination. I'm always interested in people's hobbies, and I bet your grandkids are interested in going a little more in-depth in their knowledge of what you're especially interested in.

Hobbies give you an opportunity to pass on knowledge, to share an experience, and convey a spiritual truth or tell part of your faith story. So many hobbies can be connected to a scripture and can become an object lesson with just the slightest imagination. If the person who taught you your hobby or who got you interested in it is a Christ-follower, then you can use that relationship to tell what spiritual truths you learned from that mentor.

Using the hobby as an object lesson or to connect to a scripture may be a little more foreign to most of you. Let me give you several examples where a hobby can give you an opportunity to open your Bible with your grandchild.

Sewing

Ecclesiastes 3:7 speaks of a time to sew and a time to tear apart. There are times in life when we work at coming together, and other times when we need to go our separate ways in order for God's will to be done. Acts 9:36–43 talks about Dorcus making garments for the poor. When have you used your sewing skills to help someone? Share that with your grandchild.

Fishing

In Matthew 4:19 Jesus says that He will make us fishers of men. Share with your grandchild how you have shared the message of Jesus with someone.

Bird Watching

Psalm 50:11 says that all the birds of the mountains belong to God. Everything is His, as well as each of us.

Pottery

Isaiah 64:8 says that we are the clay, and God is the potter. Talk to your grandchildren about how God will mold them through their experiences to be and to do what He has designed for them.

Woodworking

Mark 6:3 identifies Jesus as a carpenter. Don't hesitate to share with your grandchild how awesome it is to connect with Jesus, as you think about Him working with wood, making a piece of furniture or something that would help His family or neighbors do their work more easily.

Gardening

Isaiah 58:11 says that we will be like a well-watered garden when we allow God to guide us. Talk to your grandchildren about the things that give them a good environment to grow in the Lord—committing to getting into the Word of God, pouring out their hearts in conversations with the Lord, and worshiping Him passionately.

A grandfather approached me after the closing of a conference to tell me how important his hobby of tinkering at his workbench was to his relationship with his grandkids. He shared that when they were little, he took them to the basement, and they played at his feet as he worked. When they were a little older, he showed them how to use some of the tools, especially teaching them how to whittle. As the slivers of wood were tediously carved from the surface, he repeatedly told them that God had a plan for their life. "If we went to the basement, they knew they were going to get that message through the whittling." God would reveal His plan little by little, whittle by whittle. He wanted it to soak in that when they looked at this piece of wood, no one could see what it was eventually going to look like, but God knew. Through the events of their lives, God would reveal Himself. I was blessed when this grandfather shared that because of his whittling, his grandchildren (now teenagers and young adults) often would ask if they could go to the basement when they had something on their hearts, when they needed to talk to someone confidentially, and when they needed to join with someone in prayer.

How can you connect your hobby with a spiritual truth that will grab your grandchild's attention?

1. _____

2. _____

3. _____

Music

Music is a powerful way of expressing emotions and identifying where you are spiritually. I'm sure you have heard or sung along to a song that you thought was written specifically about you. How did the writer know what you were going through? How did he know what you were thinking? The words were comforting. Or, maybe they were challenging. Music has a way of saying what you don't exactly know how to say—putting words to a tune that communicates so well what you feel at that moment.

Ever since my diagnosis—wherever I go and whoever I speak with—people seem to make a similar comment. They'll tell me how strong and brave I am, often adding that they wish they could face life's challenges the way I do. When I was in my 20s and 30s, they would tell me how amazingly I handled my situation for such a young woman. I wasn't like that all the time, though. I wasn't strong all the time. I got tired. The reality is that when I'm alone and the pain is consuming, I cry out to God and melt before Him. One day I heard a song called "The Warrior is a Child" by Twila Paris. It put into words exactly what I wanted to tell people. I felt like it was written about and for me.

Lately I've been winnin'
Battles left and right
But even winners can
Get wounded in the fight
People say that I'm amazin'
Strong beyond my years
They don't see inside of me
I'm hidin' all the tears

They don't know
That I go runnin' home
When I fall down

They don't know who picks me up
When no one is around
I drop my sword
And cry for just awhile
(Look up for a smile)
'Cause deep inside this armor
The warrior is a child

Unafraid because His armor is the best
But even soldiers need
A quiet place to rest
People say that I'm amazin'
Never face retreat
They don't see the enemy
Can lay me at his feet*

My husband has that song on his playlist of favorites, because it reminds him of what we've been through together. It describes me to him through music.

Our grandkids, especially the girls, love to have music playing, so Big Pa often pulls up songs off his playlist and blasts them in the backyard or wherever we are. When this song comes up, it's a great open door to share part of Silly Grandma's story—that although I seem brave and all pulled together most of the time like a warrior, there are times when I crumble and cry like a hurt child at God's feet.

Music has the remarkable ability to say what is difficult for you to put into words.

A certain song can also be a marker that goes with a special memory. Maybe it's the song being played when you marched yourself down to the altar and claimed Jesus as your personal Savior. That makes it a special song to you and one that you can share with your grandkids. Perhaps it was a song you sang that always closed the church service when you were growing up, and it reminds you of Sunday evenings spent together with the family of God. Whatever the song, use it to share your spiritual story with your precious grandkids.

Don't forget to ask your grandkids what song means a lot to them. And, listen for why it means so much. Their part in God's story is just beginning.

What songs connect with your spiritual story?

1. _____

2. _____

3. _____

Note or Letter

As I sit here, I can't think of anything that has a bigger impact on sharing your spiritual story than writing a note or a letter. I loved having pen pals when I was in junior and senior high school. I'm a note writer. When someone comes to my mind, many times I stop what I'm doing and write them a note. When I tell someone that I'll be praying for them, I like to remind the person that I'm praying for them during the week when I'm actually following through on that commitment. When I become aware that someone is discouraged, I love to write an uplifting note, pointing out what an amazing person God created them to be. What I've found is that those people come back to me…years later…and tell me they still have that note and still frequently read it. When you write a note, you capture your thoughts and feelings in that moment and make it possible for the recipient to revisit it over and over in days to come.

Your thoughts and stories committed to pen and paper have lasting power and will have an impact long after you have left this earth and joined the heavenly community. It may seem like a bother, or something you're not good at, but years later it will have tremendous, life-changing sway. I challenge you, and encourage you greatly, to take the time today to write down what you may have difficulty saying in a conversation. There are two beauties to writing that make it more effective than verbal communication. You can think through what you want to say and choose the words that best describe your thoughts. You can let it set for a while, and then go back and tweak it to more clearly make your point. You can't do that when you're having a face-to-face conversation. There's no taking back the words that have been said. The second huge advantage is that it can be read over and over and over again. A note that was placed in a shoebox with some old photos will resurface and share its message repeatedly through the years.

When our son was six years of age, we moved back from California to live on my parents' farm. I was terribly sick, and my husband actually moved us back so there would be help with our son, and so I could die with my family around me. On Mother's Day 1987, the guys in the family went into town to attend church. I so wanted to go, because I'd watched all my growing-up years as the moms marched around the sanctuary and picked up their petunias from the windowsills. I dreamed of the day when I would get my petunia… but it wouldn't be this year. While they were gone, I asked Mom for a pencil and some paper. For some reason, on that day, Jarad's future wife was on my mind and in my prayers. Since it was Mother's Day, I wanted her to know that I had done my best to raise Jarad to love and serve God. I wanted her to know that I was thinking of her and presenting her and her parents to God, even though I never dreamed that I would live long enough to actually meet her. When the letter (and it was a long one) was finished, I placed it in an envelope, sealed it, and wrote on the outside, "To be opened by Jarad's wife-to-be on the night before their wedding." We carried that envelope around for years. To our surprise, God allowed me the awesome blessing to be there to open the envelope the night before their wedding and read the words that had been penned on those pages about 17 years earlier. Taking a few moments to write down on paper what I hoped my life said in actions has become a tremendously treasured message.

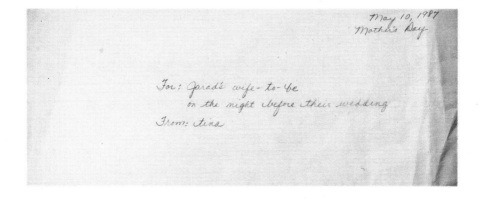

When the grandkids were born, Jarad and Kelley asked all the grandparents to write them letters individually. We each wrote our blessing that we desperately wanted God to pour over their lives. Years from now, when they go through their mementos, they will read how each grandparent desired that they have a daily walk with the Lord.

Have you written a letter or an entry in your journal that reveals something about your faith journey? Show it to your grandkids and talk about how God worked in that time. Write out what you're not confident to say in a casual conversation, so that you can talk with your grandchildren, even after you have left them physically.

Decide when you can write your thoughts down for your grandchildren:

1. I will send them a note of encouragement _____(date).

2. I will write down my hopes and dreams for them _____(date).

3. I will save a message for them to be read in the future _____(date).

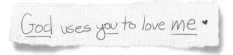

Repeated Responses

Just like hearing the multiplication facts over and over so that you'll remember them, you can intentionally incorporate certain responses into your vocabulary and conversations that will stick in your grandchild's memory. On multiple occasions, someone has responded with a phrase, and I tilted my head in a questioning manner. The person's response was, "Oh, that's something my grandma used to say all the time." Just the other day, someone asked me, "How ya doin'?" My response was, "Hangin' in like a hair in a biscuit." When I saw the strange look on their face, I added, "Oh, that's something my dad always said when someone asked him how he was doing." (I know, it sounds gross.)

So, what kind of intentional phrases and responses can you identify that have become automatic for you? Maybe you need to create some that will intentionally build a bridge to God when spoken. When you insert special phrases into your experiences and conversations, those words remind your grandkids of who you are, and who they are, in God's sight.

An intentional reminder response is when Kendall gives me a hug. I like to say to her, "Do you know what it means to me when you hug me? It's God's way of telling me that I'm loved. God uses you to love me."

Bowen is very protective of his grandmother, as well as his mother and sisters. From the time he started articulating words, he would identify himself as "Bowen, Kendall's Tector." (That's protector, if you missed it.) When Bowen helps me in an unsolicited way, I'll say, "God just used you as a helper. I thank God that He takes care of me by using you. He's given you a special gift of helping me."

Those phrases that they hear over and over don't tell a specific piece of your story, but they do remind your grandchildren of how important God is in your life as well as your desire that He be important to them.

They're not sermons. They're just 10-second reactions and reinforcements that deliver a message as if it were a sermon.

What phrases do you intentionally use to deliver a godly message? What responses can you create that will become a spiritual message to your grandchildren?

1. _____

2. _____

3. _____

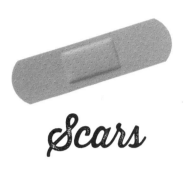

$\mathscr{Scars}$

Scars are interesting. People don't mind showing you their scars (and sometimes they're in places you'd rather not see). Kids are absolutely fascinated by scars and the crazy stories that go along with them. I think their fascination comes because they can so closely relate to cuts and accidents. Your grandkids probably already have one or two, their friends have scars, and they know that more than likely their future holds some more.

What does a scar represent? It's the mark that is left after an incident has passed. I'm well aware that there are emotional scars, but for this conversation, we're talking about the physical, I-can-see-where-it-was scars. Scars are a forever reminder that something unusual happened in your life. They bring to mind a scene, a person, a feeling, and a time of recovery.

Scars teach us. Many times, what they teach us is, "I'll never do that again!" *We had a swing set in our backyard when I was little, complete with a slide and glider. I spent a lot of time on that swing set. One particular day, I was inventing all kinds of maneuvers on the slide. After coming down every way I could think of in the upright position, I thought it would be fun to try coming down on my stomach. I wrapped my arms around the sliding board and slid down head first. Well…I didn't slide down all the way. About half-way down, my arm caught on the long screw that was sticking out the back side of the slide and ripped my arm open from one side to the other. I still have a prominent scar on my forearm to remind me of that poor decision.*

Scars can be personal trophies. *The first surgery I had was possibly going to be an amputation of my left leg. Instead, the surgeon decided to do 11 surgeries in three months, removing more of my leg each time he went in. Although the opening was around eight inches long, the scar that was left is only about an inch. God's healing and restoring power was obvious as He created me a new leg. When I look at my foot, I am reminded of a time when we got through something together—God and me. That scar represents God's power demonstrated in my body. It's a trophy that reminds me that God is full of surprises, that I am not in control, and that I can trust Him in anything. When you receive a trophy, you want to raise it up in the air and scream, "Yes! We did it!" and that's exactly how I felt once the leg was healed.*

You can use your scars to tell your grandkids of the companionship you felt with God during that time. Give them confidence in the healing power of God. Use your scars to prepare them for the time when they, too, will receive this unique kind of trophy as they walk with God.

Jesus took his scars to heaven with Him. I wonder if He looks at them as a reminder of how much He loves us. I wonder if He rubs His hands when He sees us heading the wrong direction. My scars are nothing compared to His…and that's something you can share with your grandkids.

What scars do you have that you can use to relate a spiritual truth?

1. _____

2. _____

3. _____

Science Experiment

I don't believe I've ever met a kid (or adult, for that matter) who doesn't enjoy science experiments. Kids may not understand the "why" behind them, but science is fascinating and so much fun. You can share the experience of a science experiment and make it the jumping-off point for a spiritual conversation.

Unfortunately, peers and family members are quick to hand out labels... and many times those labels are hurtful. One day out of the blue, you become the "dumb kid," the "clumsy kid," the "sissy kid," the "kid with the big nose," or the "hyper kid." The hurtful thing is that those labels stick, and they keep causing pain. They are a constant reminder that you are not enough—not good enough. You are not accepted. Did you have one of those labels when you were growing up? Or maybe you even feel as an adult that you still have a label. You can share this with a grandchild who is in one of two positions: (1) He has been the recipient of a hurtful label; or (2) She has a bad habit of passing out labels to others. You can use this science experiment to share that part of your story of faith.

Start a conversation by doing this super simple science experiment.* You'll need six M&Ms, one of each of the colors. Place all 6 M&Ms in a bowl, with the "M" side up. Position the candies toward the center of the bowl. Now, slowly pour some warm water down the side of the bowl to cover the candies. Do not pour the water on top of the candies. Just let the water rise around them until they are submerged. Then...WATCH! The colors will bleed, but that's not what you're watching for. In a few minutes, you'll see something crazy happen. The "M" will lift off the candy and float on the surface of the water.

Look, what happened! The label is no longer on the candy. And, that's the way God sees us. The Bible tells us in Galatians 3:28 (NIrv), *There is no Jew or Gentile. There is no slave or free person. There is no male or female. That's because you are all one in Christ Jesus.*

God doesn't see us with labels on. He doesn't even pay attention to what country we're from, or if we're rich or poor. In His sight, there are no labels. We are all His creation. He wants all of us to believe in and live for Jesus, no matter how other people may want to label us.

Build memories when you share some simple science experiments with your grandkids, and then watch for a way you can connect a message to that experiment that will help you share your Jesus story.

What science experiments could you use to start a spiritual conversation?

1. _____

2. _____

3. _____

*Check out *Beakers, Bubbles, and the Bible* (volumes 1 & 2) for more science experiments by Tina.

Serving

My experience tells me that there is no stronger, more effective way to see into the heart of people and get to know them better than by serving others together. Your grandkids need to be able to see a world where they are not the center of all attention. As you work together with your grandchildren, you can guide them through an array of questions and circumstances that could possibly break their little hearts as they serve those in need. Again, intentionality is a key to making this happen. Some opportunities come to your door, but with most, you need to seek out the details of how you can join a group in serving.

I spent the afternoon with my granddaughter serving others in some fun ways. We made puppets for the preschool kids at church, so each one of them would have their own—for singing, praying, and answering questions. It's a simple process of using hot glue to adhere a pair of big wiggle eyes onto dollar store dust mitts. (By the way, the dollar store will also have the wiggle eyes.)

Then we painted a piece of foam core to prep it for becoming a bush. The bush was needed as a prop for the group storytelling time.

What a great time together, and it was totally about doing something for others. The bonus was that I got to expose Kendall to some new experiences—working with foam core, painting a large area, and using a hot glue gun. As we worked, I made sure that Kendall understood how these tasks were going to make it easier for other kids to know about God.

You probably have your favorite ways to serve. Think about how you could involve your grandchild as you do. A few of you may not be aware of the organizations that are perfect for grandparent/grandchild volunteering, but here are a few that are available:

Dress a Girl Around the World. Make very simple dresses that are sent to little girls all around the world. It's the perfect way to introduce your grandchild to the skill of sewing. Check out this site online: Dressagirlaroundtheworld.com.

Feed My Starving Children. The experience you'll have is phenomenal. There are special packing times where you and your grandchild can hand-pack meals that will help prevent or reverse undernutrition. It's also a great way to talk about sanitary precautions. Fmsc.org is their website.

I've written a resource called *Unwrapping the Servant* that is loaded with ideas of how you and your grandchild can serve others. Start looking at opportunities through the lens of an activity you can do alongside your grandchild. Instead of saying, "You could do this," think, "We could do this."

It's certainly beneficial to be intentional, but don't overlook the spontaneous ways you can serve others as you're out and about with them. Keep your eyes open to how you can model serving. On the other hand, be quick to tell them about times when someone else has served you and how it made you feel.

I'd just completed a week of shopping, and the grocery cart was full. A total stranger stopped his pickup truck behind my Jeep and jumped out. He told me, "Here, let me take care of this." He proceeded to unload every bag and put them in the back of my car. I was beyond grateful! Use this kind of story to remind your grandkids how to serve others and what an impact it makes on other people. That willing man made my day. I was almost in tears.

As you experience serving together, talk about how serving others has changed your life. How has serving helped you see things differently? Why does God want us to serve each other? All the while, you'll be teaching your grandchild new skills, helping them understand the why, how, and what of difficult situations, and molding his or her heart to the mandate from Jesus to love others.

How could you serve with your grandchild?

1. _____

2. _____

3. _____

Jewelry

When I've talked with people about story starters for spiritual conversations, a frequent idea they have is to use jewelry. My family never spent money on "good" jewelry—my mom and grandmothers never wore much—so it hadn't occurred to me that you could use jewelry as a faith story starter.

I thought about it and was surprised to realize that a few things came to mind quickly. *The first piece of jewelry that came to mind was the perfect attendance pin I received one year. Each year when promotion Sunday rolled around, the Sunday school superintendent presented all those who hadn't missed a Sunday all year with a pin. They gave them out to all ages. The first year you were presented with a pin, and subsequent years you received a charm to attach to it that was inscribed with the year. I remember being awestruck when a man walked across the platform to receive another charm. He hadn't missed a Sunday in 25 years! His commitment to being at church every week was such an admirable quality. I just wanted to make it through one year and receive my pin. That seemed like an almost impossible achievement, even though my family attended almost every Sunday. I was successful for one year, but never was able to add any charms.*

A Sunday school attendance pin could be a nice stepping stone into a conversation with your grandchild about how important it is to be with the family of God—your spiritual family.

There's a cross necklace my mother gave me when I was 13. It has a tiny diamond chip in the middle that had been in a piece of jewelry she had gotten from her mother. My thirteenth year is also when I started my relationship with Jesus. I hardly took that necklace off when I was a teenager, because I couldn't look in any mirror without being reminded of who I now belonged to.

Another jewelry faith story starter.... *We gave our son a purity ring when he was a teenager after he told us about the commitment he made at a conference. As he pulled away in the limousine on his wedding day, he was halfway in the vehicle when he stood up again to toss the ring back to his dad. It's going to be a wonderful story starter with his kids one day.*

Jewelry can be a good starting point. Is there a necklace, a watch, a broach, or ring that conjures up memories that have spiritual significance for you? Maybe it's time to browse through your jewelry box. Make note of any piece that could be one of your intentional faith story starters.

What piece of jewelry could serve as a faith story starter for you?

1. _____

2. _____

3. _____

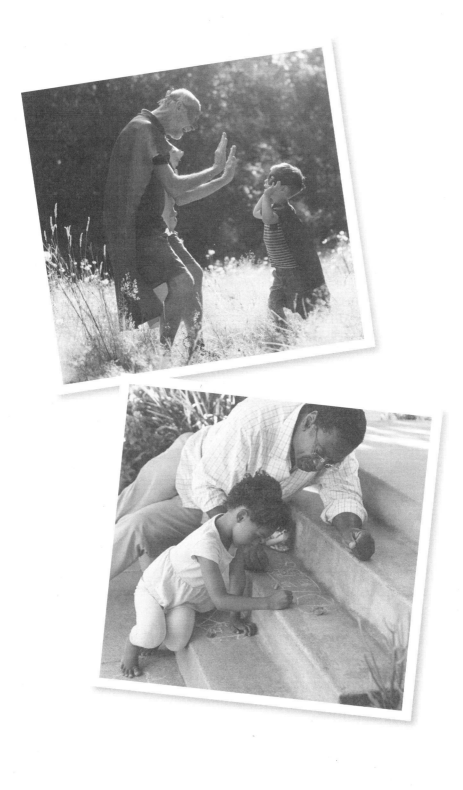

Just for Fun Activities

12 Socks of Christmas

This idea has changed as the ages of the grandkids have changed and as schedules have become more hectic. Here's the basic idea, so you can take it and make it your own.

As soon as the tree and Christmas decorations go up (that's Thanksgiving weekend for us), the 12 Socks of Christmas also go up. We have two half-walls that divide our foyer and main living room. On those walls I hang 3 pairs of socks for Kendall on one side, and 3 pairs of socks on the other wall for Bowen…12 socks in all. The very first year I did this, I actually separated the socks and hung them individually across the walls.

I plan for the kids to come over 6 times (for the 6 pairs of socks) leading up to Christmas. When they arrive, one pair of socks will have a note in it that describes what we'll be doing that visit. The child whose socks held the note takes home their new socks.

I encourage you to include a variety of things in the socks: making gifts, receiving gifts, serving others, staying home, going somewhere, activities that require a lot of energy, and calm activities.

Because my grandkids receive so many presents on Christmas morning from other relatives, I usually incorporate my gifts to them in the socks. It makes it a special time for us to enjoy and play together without the frantic, craziness of Christmas morning.

Let me share some of the things that have been in our socks. Most of the time I include more than one.

- Count the nativities in my house. (I collect nativities, and they are everywhere!)

- Candy cane hunt (with flashlights). These have been both inside and out-side. There always seems to be one candy cane that refuses to be found.

- Go to Bass Pro Shop's interactive Christmas display for kids.

- Have a fondue dinner.

- Have a Christmas tea party.

- Spend the night and get new Christmas pajamas.

- Make coated pretzels.

- Make an ornament.

- Give them clues to find their present. They usually have to find a present that's wrapped in the paper that their personal note was written on. If they find someone else's, they can't say anything.

- Watch a movie together, with hot chocolate and popcorn.

- Make hot chocolate and cookies, then deliver them to Salvation Army bell ringers. (We always get pictures with the kids and each ringer.)

- Count the change in Grandma's coin jar, then decide on a purchase in the World Vision catalog (like a chicken or pig).

- Go to SkyZone (our local trampoline park).

- Eat lunch at their favorite restaurant.

- Paint on canvas.

- Play board games all evening.

- Go to a museum that has a special Christmas display.

- Go to a puppet play.

- Make peppermint trees.

- Make a photo album, (replicating poses from when they were little).

Grocery Race

Grocery shopping can be tedious for kids. You don't have to listen intentionally at the supermarket to hear a child crying or screaming as the adult attempts to rush the cart through the aisles. Games, races, searches, and challenges can turn that around and make grocery shopping not only something that's marked off your to-do list, but a fun memory-making adventure. After you do this once, your grandkids will be asking to accompany you to the store. You may even get a text, "When do you need groceries, Grandpa?"

The Grocery Race is a little of all four—a game, a race, a search, and a challenge. Winner, winner! First of all, you need two adult shoppers, preferably Grandma and Grandpa. Randomly, assign each grandchild to a grandparent. This can be by drawing a name out of a hat, whoever rolls the first "4" on a dice gets to choose who he or she goes with, etc.

Make your master list of what you need to purchase. Divide that list into two lists, paying particular attention to give each team the same number of items and similar places around the store to get items. For instance, one team might have light bulbs (which is on the far back side of the store in electronics), and the other team might have cotton swabs (which is on the far-right front corner of the store, close to the pharmacy). Both teams will have to go to the other side of the store at some point.

Each team (grandparent and grandchild) chooses a team cart that they're happy with. No wobbly wheels or crazy squeaking. Determine the exact location your cart must be when you complete your list (such as, in front of checkout lane 7), and make sure the list is where you can access it easily. Say "Go" and the madness, I mean fun, begins! Each team will try to be the first to get everything on their list in the cart and the cart back to the determined place.

It gets pretty vigorous, so consider these preparation tips.

- Choose a low traffic time at the store.

- Check both lists to make sure they take you to similar parts of the store.

- Check both lists to make sure they are readable. (I suggest typing them out. It can be difficult to read someone else's writing, no matter how old you are.)

- Use your inhaler before beginning!

If you're a little uptight as a grandparent, you need to have a talk with your head before you begin. Enjoy, I mean *really* enjoy, this activity. Your grandchild will want you to move faster than you normally do when shopping, so be ready for a little prodding. When you can't find an item, invite other shoppers to help you find what you're looking for. Tell them what you and your grandchild are doing but make it quick.

The Result: You'll be the envy of every grandparent you talk to.

Magic Hat

A fun thing that has gone on for years at our house (and will probably continue for decades) is the Magic Hat. It's a plastic top hat that looks like one a magician would wear. It sits on its top, so it appears upside down. There are rubber flaps that close off the hole where the hat would be pulled down over the head. The Magic Hat sits on a reachable shelf in the foyer of our home.

Each time I know the grandkids are going to visit, I put something in the Magic Hat. Its contents have changed as their interest and ages have changed. When they were small, the twins were absolutely thrilled with a Cutie orange. Now, they are happy campers when there's a piece of mint gum in there. The surprise ranges from candy to stickers to fruit to clues to find something around the house (like a board game to play).

During the Christmas season, instead of the Magic Hat, I put out a 3-piece ceramic Santa train that my mom made when I was little. Each piece of the train has a lid that lifts off. They never know which car of the train will hold their surprise.

The Magic Hat is so special the grandkids race to get their coats off and hung so they can rush to see what might be in the hat.

Mystery Lunch

This is great fun for grandkids who are 4 years old and up (through adulthood)! It's a creative alternative to "having lunch together."

Place about 15 different small food items on plates or in bowls. Then cover each one with some kind of lid—inverted bowl, cloth napkin, saucer, etc.

Each person is given 100 pennies. They will bid against one another to see who gets to purchase what's under a particular lid, even though they don't know what it is. Once all items are purchased, they are free to trade with someone else (since they now know what everything is), or they can sell off portions of what they bought.

Choose items you know your crew likes, but here are some finger-friendly items we include when we're having a casual lunch.

- Cherry tomatoes
- Mini corn dogs
- Carrot sticks
- Grapes
- Cheez-Its
- Cheese cubes/slices
- Meatballs
- Broccoli & dip
- Strawberries
- Pepperonis
- Chips
- Red pepper strips
- Ritz peanut butter bits
- Blueberries
- Peanut butter & honey on crackers

Lunch becomes a fun game when you add this mystery twist. As all eat, they can continue to negotiate for items that others may still have.

Who has the most pennies when lunch is over?

Pencils of Encouragement

Kids love a brand-new pencil! That sounds crazy, that something so inexpensive can bring light into their day. Just think about the hours they spend in school, pushing a pencil across page after page of worksheets. (I hope there aren't too many, but that's a topic for another day.) How cool would it be if that pencil could actually help you build a relationship with your grandchild?

You can pick up a brightly colored pencil box at most dollar stores. Then, you'll need a supply of plain pencils, along with a black ultra-fine tip marker. With your steadiest hand, write a different word of encouragement on each pencil. I've listed some, but I challenge you to think of some encouraging statements that speak directly to the talents and skills of your grandchild. Don't put an age on this gift. Every age can use a new pencil…or two…or 12!

As a bonus, spend a little together time with your grandchildren when you give this to them. Provide a supply of letter stickers, flat-back rhinestones, permanent markers, and other craft supplies. Encourage them to decorate their pencil box, not forgetting that their name should be central.

Consider using some of these encouraging declarations.

- You are a rock star to me!
- You can do this.
- I'm so glad you're my grandkid.
- Always rely on God.
- There's not a day when I'm not proud of you.
- Got a problem? You and God can solve it!

- God knew you before you were born.
- You are a masterpiece.
- You…amazing…'nuff said.
- I love to watch you dance.
- You're a great problem solver.
- You are incredible at math. Look out!
- You are so talented.
- Have a fantastic day!
- I love your creativity.
- You're the best.
- My life is better because of you.
- You are so intelligent.
- Your laugh is like magic.
- Follow God's plan for you.
- I'm praying for you every day.
- You are so important.
- I love you bunches.
- Being with you is the best.
- You are a champion.

What other encouraging statements would you write on pencils to your grandchildren?

1. _____

2. _____

3. _____

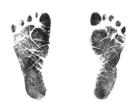

Repose Infant Photos

Have you ever given your cell phone to a grandchild and they go straight to your photos? It happens to me all the time. A finger will swipe, swipe, swipe across the screen until there are no more photos, and then they swipe back the other way. When they come across a short video I made of them, they're glued to it, and then immediately hit the "play" button for a second round. And, it doesn't stop at two times. They'll watch that same video indefinitely. Yeah, kids love pictures of themselves.

Let the grandchildren choose their favorite pictures from when they were much younger. The object will be to recreate the pose and background of the photos they choose. Don't succumb to the temptation to prepare everything for your grandkids. Much of the fun is in figuring out how you're going to make it happen. As they examine the pictures closely, they'll realize, "We still have that blanket. I know exactly where it is." Once you have gone through all the chosen photos, everyone should have a list of what they'll bring to the photo shoot. I print out the old picture for use at the photo shoot, because it gives us a bigger reference as we pose. Before moving to recreate the next photo, always check the one you have taken alongside the original old one. Does the new photo remind you of the old one?

We uploaded old and new photos and designed a photo album on a photo-designing website. Any time your grandkids can play with the computer, you have earned brownie points, so including them in the design of the album is a must. This particular album became a Christmas gift for their mother.

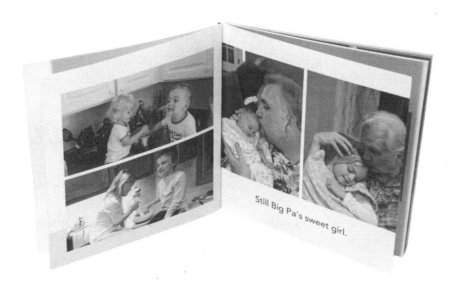

Still Big Pa's sweet girl.

This together time takes a few sessions and, truthfully, it's a lot of work… but fun work! Throughout these times, the doors are wide open for conversation and relationship building. It's the perfect time to talk about the changes you have seen in your grandchildren. Convey how they were created in the image of God, and that He will continue to mold them as they submit to Him.

Describe some photos that you would enjoy recreating with your grandchildren.

1. _____

2. _____

3. _____

Road Trip Scavenger Hunt

Recall from your young days the games you played on a road trip. Many of them had to do with looking out the windows to notice things that were outside the car—on billboards, in fields, on vehicles that passed in the next lane. At one time, we created a road trip Bingo for all the passengers, and each person attempted to be the first to find five things in a row. Then, there was the alphabet game, where you had to find a word on a sign that began with each letter of the alphabet, in order.

This is a version of the alphabet game, on steroids and with technology. If you're traveling with grandkids, they will love this distraction. Each grandchild will need an iPad or cell phone to take pictures. Beforehand, make a piece of paper with all the letters of the alphabet on it. Give each grandchild a pencil.

The object is for each grandchild to take a photo of something that begins with one of the letters on their sheet. They don't have to go in order. (Of course, you can change the rules and make it more challenging by going in order.) Each time they take a picture connected with a letter, they will circle that specific letter to keep track of their progress.

Here's a twist that taps into their creativity. They are not necessarily trying to find words on signs that begin with those letters. Encourage them to take pictures of things they see that start with that letter (like fence for "F"). They can also describe objects using the letter as an adjective (like for "E" they could take a picture of an "Enormous sign.") By no means is this an activity for just elementary grandkids. Your grown grandchildren will love snapping these pictures, and it's a great way to pass the time while being together.

Flat Jesus

This is a fun way to stay connected with your grandkids if you do a lot of traveling. More than likely they have done something similar in school at some point.

Laminate your picture of Jesus.

Before you begin your travels, briefly talk with your grandchild about your Flat Jesus adventure. In that conversation you can emphasize that Jesus is with you no matter where you are in the world. He doesn't stay at home when you travel. This Flat Jesus is only a picture that reminds us of the real Jesus. For younger grandchildren, make sure they understand it isn't the laminated figure that will stay with you all the time (or you'll end up having to tote it with you everywhere when you get home).

When you're on the road and are in an interesting spot, pull out the Flat Jesus and snap a picture of the two of you. Send the picture to your grandchild with an update on what you saw or did in that place. If you learned something new or unusual, tell your grandchild about that. Always include a statement that emphasizes that this is another place Jesus went with you. He is always with me. He will never leave me.

Where can you take your Flat Jesus?

1. _____

2. _____

3. _____

Countdown

When there's something special coming up, share a countdown with your grandkids. It makes the coming event feel even more special. And countdowns build anticipation. Being able to wait is a great lesson that kids need to learn. In our modern society, so many things are instant. Having immediate access to entertainment, hot food, and knowledge is ingrained in our grandchildren, which makes the concept of anticipation a rare thing.

I did a countdown when we were anticipating a trip together to Washington, D.C. with our son's family. The Countdown Box was a large box that contained an envelope, bag, or package for each day leading up to our trip. I researched interesting facts about different places we were going to visit. I also found trinkets or appropriate gifts to go along with different historic sights. There were problems for the kids to figure out and things for them to do. Each day they opened one more bag. Here are a few examples of what was included in the bags for this Countdown to Vacation in Washington, D.C.

An alligator that grows when you put it in water and an alligator bubble mitt. President Herbert Hoover and President John Quincy Adams both kept alligators at the White House.

I wrote the alphabet on a grid but left out the "J". Washington, D.C.'s streets are lettered, but there is no "J" street. "J" was not a common letter yet when the streets were named.

Moon Pies for everyone. The Air and Space Museum has a rock from the moon that's on display for visitors.

Some gold stick-on stars. The World War II Memorial is one of Washington, D.C.'s newest memorials. It opened in 2004. It contains a large fountain, columns with the names of each state and territory, and 4,048 gold stars. Each of the stars represents 100 American military deaths during that war. Can you figure out how many American military deaths there were?

Tracing paper and a book about the memorial. The Vietnam Memorial has 53,318 names engraved on the wall. People often bring tracing paper and a pencil to make rubbings of names they know. Practice making a rubbing of a coin or engraving. Then, take some of the paper on the trip to make a rubbing from the Vietnam Memorial.

Call Silly Grandma. The first phone number at the White House was "1." Call Silly Grandma and tell her one thing you're excited to see on our trip.

Red, white, and blue T-shirts. Red, white, and blue are America's colors because they were used in the flag of the United States of America.

- *White* stands for purity and innocence.

- *Red* stands for hardiness and valor.

- *Blue* stands for vigilance, perseverance, and justice.

$5 bill and some hand sanitizer. The Bureau of Engraving and Printing (BEP) makes over 26 million bills a day. The largest bill ever printed was a $100,000 bill. Each day, they use 9.7 tons of ink to print the money. Almost all (95%) of the new money is used to replace old worn-out bills, which are very dirty. You should use hand sanitizer after handling money.

Rolls of toilet paper. The White House has 35 bathrooms!

Night light. There are over 400,000 service members and their families buried at Arlington Cemetery. Every day there are 25–30 funerals at the cemetery. Arlington is the gravesite of President John F. Kennedy. Two of Kennedy's children (Arabella and Patrick) and Jacqueline Bouvier Kennedy Onassis are also buried alongside the president. At his funeral on November 25, 1963, Jacqueline (wife) lit an eternal flame that remains lit today. The eternal flame has been extinguished a few times by accident. On December 10, 1963, a group of Catholic schoolchildren were sprinkling the temporary flame with holy water. The cap came off the bottle and water poured onto the flame, putting it out. A cemetery official quickly relit the flame by hand. And, in August 1967, an exceptionally heavy rain extinguished the permanent flame.

Pair of flip-flops for each of them. During World War II, the Nazis put Jewish people in prison…horrible prison camps. When they arrived at the prison camp, their shoes were taken away from them. Huge piles of shoes were found at all the prison camps when the war came to an end. The Holocaust Museum tells about how the Jewish people were treated during WWII. On the second floor of the Museum, you will enter a darkened room that is filled with shoes. Old shoes. New shoes. Worn shoes. Badly repaired shoes. Some were withered with use. Some were scuffed from extensive use. Black leather shoes. Brown cloth shoes. Men's shoes. Women's shoes. Wide shoes. Narrow shoes. Baby shoes. Hundreds of them. They are arranged in a heap 10–12 inches deep covering the 200 square foot floor except for a narrow path that you walk through to go to the next room. Shoes.

A book for each of them. The Library of Congress is the largest library in the U.S. It has one of the 3 perfect copies of the Gutenberg Bible. There are more than 100,000 comic books in the library. It has every single public tweet ever made on Twitter. More than 50 million tweets are collected every day. The library spends $100,000 on light bulbs each year. Only members of Congress or their staff are allowed to check out books. Every day they add about 11,000 new books to the Library. There are 33 million books in the Library of Congress that are written in 460 different languages. It takes 883 miles of shelving to hold them.

A talking toy sheep that repeats back whatever you say. President Woodrow Wilson had sheep on the front lawn of the White House. They were used to mow the grass and then they sold the wool to make money to donate to the Red Cross.

Lego set of the Lincoln Memorial. The Lincoln Memorial Association was created just two years after President Abraham Lincoln was assassinated in 1865, but because of squabbling about the details, it wasn't actually constructed until 1914. The statue of the President was originally supposed to be 10 feet tall, but before completion it had been changed to 19 feet. There is a typo in the inscription. FUTURE is actually spelled EUTURE. Lincoln was an advocate for sign language and authorized the creation of a school for the deaf. The sculptor changed Lincoln's hand position to include A and L in sign language. It was also the site where Martin Luther King Jr. made his famous "I Have a Dream" speech in 1963.

Documenting the trip with new iPads. You need to capture all the interesting things we'll get to do on our trip to Washington, D.C. You have learned some unique facts about D.C. through this countdown, but there's much more waiting. With this gift you'll be able to journal your experiences each day—with words, photos, and videos.

Another countdown we do each year is a New Year's Countdown. Our first "midnight celebration" actually happened at 8:00, but as the grandkids got older, midnight got a little later each year. Balloons are blown up with a slip of paper inside that tells what they'll be doing that half-hour. On the outside of the balloon, a time is written with a permanent black marker that tells when it should be opened. You can include:

• Hors d'oeuvres

• Glow-in-the-dark baths

• Dance time where we replace a regular bulb with a strobe bulb and turn out the lights

• Play a game, like Pie in the Face

• Figure out an Escape Room hunt that uses clues to lead the participants through the house to find a prize

• Play Bean Boozled

• Have an indoor snowball fight

• Wear crazy hats and get out the noisemakers as they watch a countdown video

What big event could you create a countdown for your grandkids?

1. _____

2. _____

3. _____

Fondue

You want an interactive way to have a meal? I never dreamed the grand-kids would enjoy fondue so much, though they do love cheese. Being able to choose their colored skewer and what they would dip into the pot was a fabulous experience. If your fondue pot didn't come with colored skewers, you can get wooden skewers in the kitchen gadget area at any discount store. No one wanted to stop eating! We've done both a cheese fondue and a chocolate dessert fondue.

Cut fruits, vegetables, breads, and meats into bite-size pieces. If you have a Lazy Suzanne for your table, serving the fondue is much easier. Each person chooses a "bite" and stabs it onto their skewer. Then, cover your bite by dipping it as far as you like into the melted cheese or chocolate. We all ended up leaning over our table to reach the fondue pot. Eyes lit up at the new encounter, and we all had a blast eating our entire dinner this way.

Chocolate Fondue
- 10 ounces of milk chocolate almond bark
- ½ c. half & half

Cut chocolate bark into very small pieces. Put the bark and the half & half in the fondue pot and melt slowly. Keep stirring it. You can actually turn the pot off while you dip, because it will stay relatively thin for quite a while.

Things to dip in chocolate: strawberries, marshmallows, pound cake, pretzels, peanut butter wafers, blackberries, mandarin oranges.

Cheese Fondue

- 1 c. Monterey jack cheese
- 1 c. cheddar cheese, shredded
- 1 c. Swiss cheese
- 1 c. American cheese
- 3 tablespoons flour
- 2 cup chicken stock
- ¼ t. garlic powder
- ¼ t. onion powder

In medium bowl, toss cheeses and flour to mix. Place chicken stock in 2-quart saucepan; cook over medium heat until very hot. Add cheese mixture ½ cup at a time, stirring until melted. Cook until very warm. Stir in garlic powder. Pour into fondue pot.

Things to dip in the cheese: meatballs, pieces of ham, smokie links, focaccia bread, broccoli, peppers, mushrooms, apple slices, cherry tomatoes.

Sharing meals is something the Bible speaks of frequently. The Passover meal was extremely important to God's people. Communion was initiated around the dinner table. Mary and Martha prepared a meal for Jesus.

When you come together for the purpose of a meal, it becomes not only physical, but spiritual. Eating a meal filled with laughter and caring conversations restores and refocuses. It's a time when you hit the "pause" button and eat together, something we do more often by ourselves but that has great benefit when done together. The shared meal is almost a lost discipline. Don't pass up the experience of sharing meals with your grandkids.